Mountain Biking Bozeman

WILL HARMON

(Formerly *Fat Trax: Bozeman*)

Guilford, Connecticut
An imprint of The Globe Pequot Press

A FALCON GUIDE®

Previously published by Falcon Publishing, Inc.

Cover photo by Cheyenne Rouse.

Cataloging-in-Publication Data is on file at the Library of Congress.

Manufactured in Canada
First edition/Second printing

CAUTION

Outdoor recreational activities are by their very nature potentially hazardous. All participants in such activities must assume the responsibility for their own actions and safety. The information contained in this guidebook cannot replace sound judgment and good decision-making skills, which help reduce the risk exposure, nor does the scope of this book allow for disclosure of all the potential hazards and risks involved in such activities.

Learn as much as possible about the outdoor recreational activitiesin which you participate, prepare for the unexpected, and be cautious. The reward will be a safer and more enjoyable experience.

 Text pages printed on recycled paper.

Contents

Acknowledgments

I spent a season riding solo on the trails in this book—but was never alone, thanks to a supportive team of friends and family.

Special thanks go to Ernie and Stana Loneman and Didi Eitel for a place to crash for the night, after a day of crashing on the trails.

Dave Cary, recreation planner for the Bozeman Ranger District on the Gallatin National Forest, pointed me to the best rides. His annotated map saved me days of exploratory wandering. He also reviewed—and provided facts for—the ride descriptions.

Chris Saboda and the crew at Bangtail Bikes and the staff at MSU's Outdoor Recreation Program offered good advice and handy map access.

My bike is still alive and functioning thanks to parts and repairs from Jim Barnes and his team at Big Sky Cyclery, and Eric Grove and the gang at Great Divide Cyclery, both in Helena.

The ever-patient staffs at the State Library and Lewis and Clark County Library, both in Helena, will be relieved that yet another book is done and I'll be out of their hair for a few months. I hope it didn't take too long to put all the maps back where they belonged.

Also thanks to Randall Green and Bill Schneider at Falcon Press for making this a value-added, made-in-Montana project.

Rose, Evan, and Ben were the best camping buddies I could ask for, especially when we woke up to a quarter inch of frozen rain on the tent (and everything else) at Langohr.

Finally, thanks to all the people I met on the trail who so generously shared their knowledge of Bozeman's backcountry. Some riders clam up when asked about their favorite trails, but the folks I met couldn't keep their enthusiasm bottled in. This book is much the better for it.

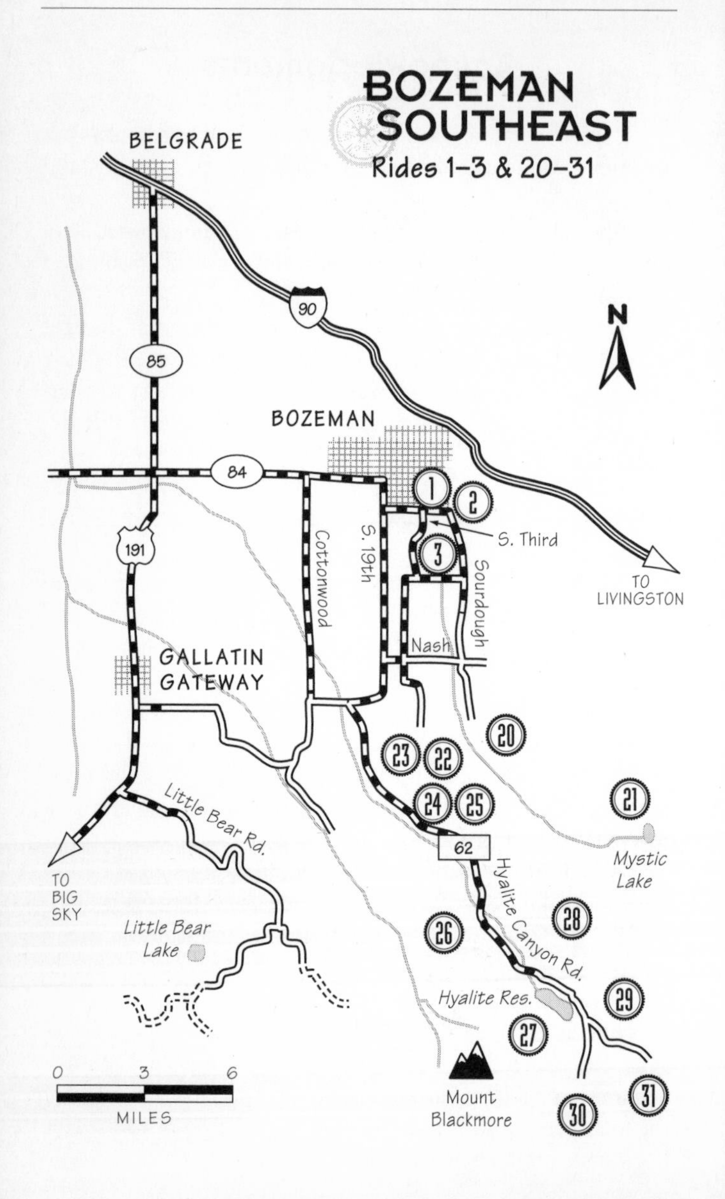
BOZEMAN
SOUTHEAST
Rides 1–3 & 20–31
BELGRADE
90
85
BOZEMAN
84
191
Cottonwood
S. 19th
S. Third
Sourdough
Nash
TO
LIVINGSTON
GALLATIN
GATEWAY
1
2
3
20
21
22
23
24
25
26
27
28
29
30
31
62
Little Bear Rd.
Hyalite Canyon Rd.
Mystic
Lake
TO
BIG
SKY
Little Bear
Lake
Hyalite Res.
Mount
Blackmore
0
3
6
MILES
N

BOZEMAN NORTH

Rides 4–19

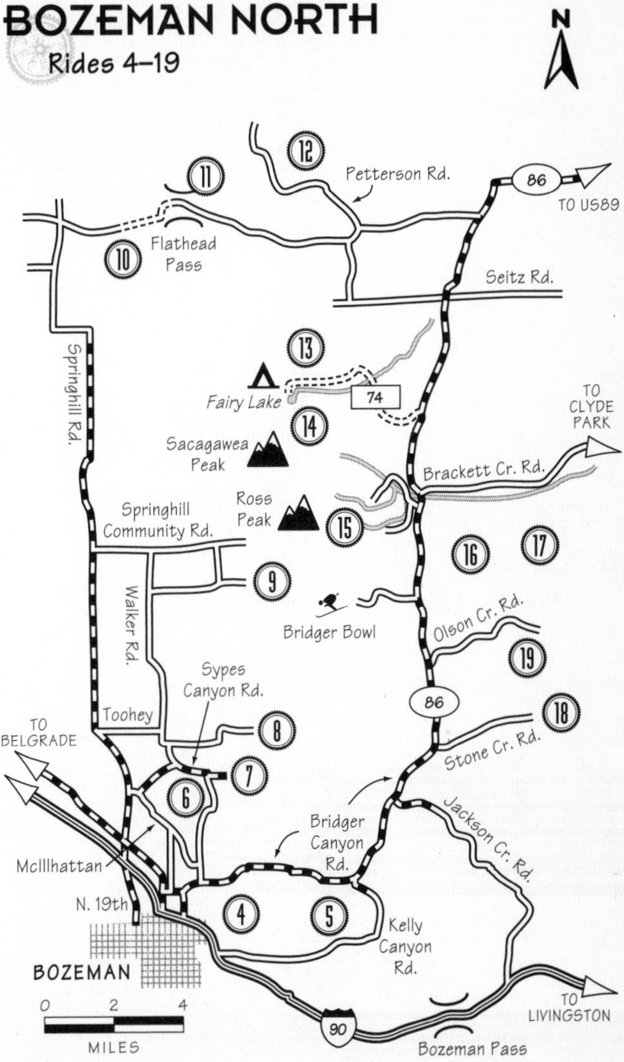

N

12
11
Petterson Rd.
86
TO US89
Flathead Pass
10
Seitz Rd.
Springhill Rd.
13
Fairy Lake
74
14
TO CLYDE PARK
Sacagawea Peak
Brackett Cr. Rd.
Ross Peak
Springhill Community Rd.
15
16
17
9
Walker Rd.
Bridger Bowl
Olson Cr. Rd.
19
Sypes Canyon Rd.
86
Toohey
18
TO BELGRADE
8
Stone Cr. Rd.
7
6
Jackson Cr. Rd.
Bridger Canyon Rd.
McIlhattan
N. 19th
4
5
Kelly Canyon Rd.
BOZEMAN
0 2 4
MILES
90
TO LIVINGSTON
Bozeman Pass

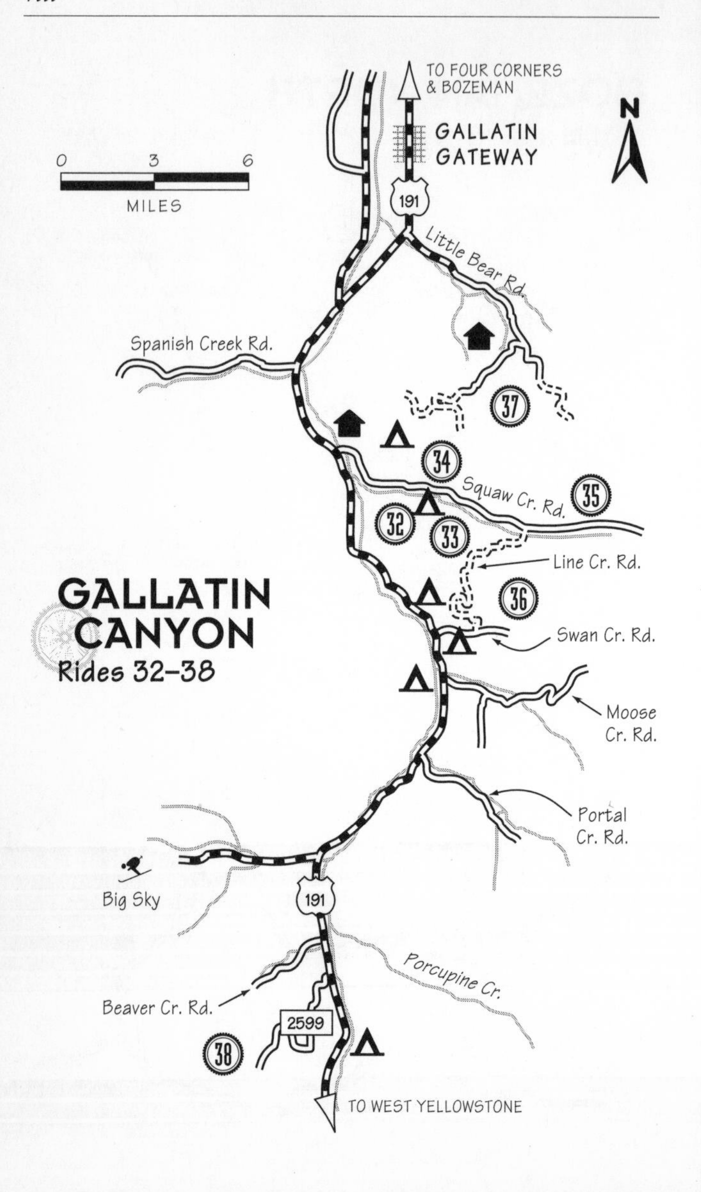

TO FOUR CORNERS
& BOZEMAN
GALLATIN
GATEWAY
N
0
3
6
MILES
191
Little Bear Rd.
Spanish Creek Rd.
37
34
Squaw Cr. Rd.
35
32
33
Line Cr. Rd.
36
GALLATIN
CANYON
Rides 32–38
Swan Cr. Rd.
Moose
Cr. Rd.
Portal
Cr. Rd.
Big Sky
191
Porcupine Cr.
Beaver Cr. Rd.
2599
38
TO WEST YELLOWSTONE

USGS TOPO MAP INDEX

N

			Blacktail Mtn.	Hatfield Mtn.		
Logan	Nixon Gulch	Horseshoe Creek	Flathead Pass	Sacagawea Peak	Sedan	Wilsall
Manhattan SW	Manhattan	Belgrade	Miser Creek	Saddle Peak	Grassy Mtn.	Gobblers Knob
Madison Plateau	Anceney	Bozeman Hot Springs	Bozeman	Kelly Creek	Bozeman Pass	Hoppers
Cherry Creek Canyon	Ruby Mtn.	Gallatin Gateway	Wheeler Mtn.	Mt. Ellis	Bald Knob	Chimney Rock
Willow Swamp	Beacon Point	Garnet Mtn.	Mt. Blackmore	Friday Peak	Big Draw	Pray
Lone Mtn.	Gallatin Peak	Hidden Lake	The Sentinel	Lewis Creek	Daily Lake	Emigrant
Sphinx Mtn.	Ousel Falls	Lone Indian Peak	Ramshorn Peak	Miner	Dome Mtn.	Monitor Peak

90
86
90
191

MAP LEGEND

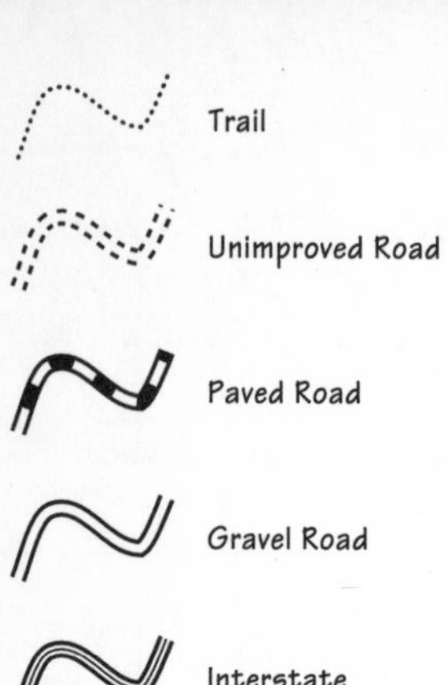

Trail

Unimproved Road

Paved Road

Gravel Road

Interstate

Wilderness Boundary

Waterway

State Line

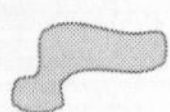

Lake/Reservoir

Cliff

Camping

Town

City

Trailhead

Route Marker

Mountain Peak (Overview map)

Parking

Mile Marker

Interstate

U.S. Highway

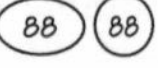

State Highway

Forest Road

Gate

Building

Preface

Notes from a Reformed Bozemaniac

This book was supposed to be a simple compilation of the best mountain bike rides around Bozeman, Montana. Those rides are, in fact, found in these pages. But in the course of reconnoitering them during one long season I couldn't resist recording some overtly personal details in the mile-by-mile descriptions.

There's mile 2.0 on the Sypes Canyon trail, breaking onto the open ridge high above town, with bright yellow arrowleaf balsam root blazing in the sun. The same sweet July breeze greeted me there 14 years ago when I first pedaled a proto-mountain bike up that grade.

There's also the smooth, sinuous singletrack through deep forest on the north end of Grassy Mountain. And the back-of-beyond picnic spot reserved for trials riders, endorphin junkies and other crazies willing to take a tough detour from the History Rock Loop.

These are the features and qualities that beckoned me back to trails I first rode on a touring bike back in 1979. In 1982 an upgrade to a genuine mountain bike opened up new terrain, including Hyalite Divide and a first ascent of Sacagawea Peak by bicycle (an exercise in absurdity—the peak belongs to hikers, migratory eagles, and the near-constant westerlies).

Back then, fat tire flyers were rare enough to grab headlines in the *Chronicle*. Imagine Bozeman with only six mountain bikes prowling the streets! (Make that four—at least two were generally in the shop for damage control.)

Now Bozeman swarms with rock-shocked, aerospace-alloyed, bullhorn-handlebarred bikes. But one thing that hasn't changed much since those early years is the strong sense of camaraderie on the trails. And not just among bikies.

In more than 500 miles of "field research" for this book, I met countless hikers, runners, horseback riders, hunters, anglers, motorbikers, four-wheelers, bird watchers, rock climbers, loggers, game wardens, and even babies in strollers. Every encounter was friendly, some even heartwarming. We would all dance off trail to yield right-of-way to each other—then we'd talk for 20 minutes, share snacks, and compare notes on our favorite trails.

The Bozeman backcountry is the friendliest place I've ever spun a granny gear. That's a tradition worth saving. You may not have the time or inclination to visit for 20 minutes with each passerby, but a smile and a friendly hello help spread good vibes and goodwill up and down the trail.

Of course, trail etiquette and treading lightly involve more than just smiling at your neighbors—check out the International Mountain Bicycling Association's "Rules of the Trail" on page 5. A little common courtesy and respect for fellow trail users goes a long way toward preserving the peace. And peaceable trails are *open* trails.

So pick a ride, strap on that high-tech brain bucket, and head for the hills!

Will Harmon
January, 1996

Get Ready to CRANK!

Where to ride? It's a quandary that faces every mountain biker, beginner or expert, local or expatriate.

If you're new to the area, where do you start? If you're a long-time local, how do you avoid the rut of riding the same old trails week after week? And how do you find new terrain that's challenging but not overwhelming? Or an easier ride for when your not-so-serious buddies want to come along?

Welcome to *Mountain Biking Bozeman*. Here are nearly 40 rides ranging from easy road routes to smooth singletrack to bravado-busting boulder fields. The rides are described in plain language, with accurate distances and ratings for physical and technical difficulty. Each entry offers a wealth of detailed information that's easy to read and use, from an armchair or on the trail.

Our aim is three-fold: to help you choose a ride that's appropriate for your fitness and skill level; to make it easy to find the trailhead; and to help you complete the ride safely, without getting lost. Take care of these basics and fun is bound to break loose.

The Bozeman Backcountry: What to Expect

The rides in this book cover a wide variety of terrain, but most are in the mountains. That means two things: the trails are often steep and rough, and the weather can be unpredictable and, at times, severe.

Mountain terrain requires preparedness. Get in good shape before you attempt these rides, and know your limits. Clean and maintain your bike frequently. Before each ride, check tires, rims, brakes, handlebars, seat, shifters, derailleurs, and chain to make sure they survived the last ride and are functioning properly.

A helmet is essential for safe mountain biking; it can save your life and prevent serious injuries. Cycling gloves are another essential piece of safety equipment that can save hands from cuts and bruises from falls, encroaching branches, and rocks. They also improve your grip and comfort on the handlebars.

Always pack at least one (filled) water bottle. A snack such as fruit or sports energy bars can keep those mighty thighs cranking for extra hours and prevent dreaded "bonk"—the sudden loss of energy when your body runs out of fuel. Dress for the weather and pack a wind- and water-proof jacket "just in case." Don't forget sunglasses, sunscreen, lip balm, and insect repellent, as needed.

I tend to go light on tools, but a pump and tube patch kit can save you from a long walk, or, on longer rides, a night out. A few allen wrenches for tightening or adjusting seat posts, handlebars, chainrings, pedals, brake posts, and other components can likewise make the difference between a disaster and a five-minute pit stop. Some folks aren't comfortable unless they bring 20 pounds of tools; you can hear them rattling up the trail, but they're rarely stranded by mechanical problems.

This book is designed to be easily carried in a pocket or bike bag, and the maps and ride descriptions will help anyone unfamiliar with the trails. U.S. Geological Survey topographic maps can provide a more detailed view of the terrain, but ride routes may not be shown. The correct topo maps are listed for each ride.

Finally—I'll say it again—always wear a helmet.

Bozeman's **weather** spans the gamut of North American extremes, particularly in the surrounding mountains. Snow can fall any day of the year, but summer highs may top 100 degrees Fahrenheit. In general, higher elevations are cooler (by as much as 10 degrees for every 1,000 feet) and windier. If you drive to a trailhead, play it safe and take a variety of clothes in the car to match the weather you're likely to encounter.

Most of the good off-road riding near Bozeman happens from mid-June through September. Some trails, particularly at higher elevations, are only ridable from late July through August. (Bear in mind that hunting seasons may overlap prime pedaling times. Check with the Montana Department of Fish, Wildlife and Parks for specific dates. See Appendix B. If you do ride during hunting season, a blaze orange vest is a sensible precaution.).

Rain or snow can turn trails to purée for days, at any time of year. Please stay off wet, muddy trails—the soil damage and erosion even one rider can cause is simply too great.

In general, the valley rides and lower trails in the west Bridgers open and dry out earliest. Be aware, however, that heavy runoff may make some stream crossings unsafe even when the adjoining trails are dry and passable. The Bangtails (with the exception of Stone Creek) also dry out slightly sooner than other areas around Bozeman. Other possible early and late season rides are the rockier trails that branch off of Hyalite Canyon Road (see rides 24, 25, 28, and 29).

The yearly number of rainy or snowy days tends to increase as you head south down the Gallatin. Many trails just north of Yellowstone National Park are more often muddy than not, limiting good riding to a handful of days, unpredictably scattered through the summer.

Because damp trails and clay-based soils are common around Bozeman, many local riders prefer open-cage pedals with toe clips as opposed to clipless style pedals. If you do ride clipless, carry an old toothbrush to clean the mud out as needed.

In winter, most Bozemaniacs limit their riding to commutes around town or an occasional foray on the frozen dirt roads beyond the 'burbs north and west of town. Better to trade wheels for hot-waxed skis and snowboards when the snow flies.

Rules of the Trail

French writer Albert Camus once said, "Rules require of us no integrity." In other words, obey the rules and save yourself the trouble of all that moral soul-searching.

Catch the irony? Camus wasn't speaking in favor of rules. He was lamenting the fact that rules tend to proliferate and shrivel our consciences.

So before I introduce a rather firm set of rules for mountain bikers, let me explain my corollary to Camus' adage. "Integrity," I submit, "has no need for rules."

If every mountain biker always yielded the right-of-way, stayed on the trail, avoided wet or muddy trails, never cut switchbacks, never skidded, always rode in control, showed respect for other trail users, and carried out every last scrap of what was carried in (candy wrappers and bike-part debris included)—in short, if we all *did the right thing*—we wouldn't need a list of rules governing our behavior.

Fact is, most mountain bikers are conscientious and are trying to do the right thing. Most of us own that integrity. (No one becomes good at something as demanding and painful as grunting up sheer mountainsides by cheating.)

Most of us don't need rules.

But we do need knowledge of what exactly *is* the right thing to do?

Here are some guidelines—I like to think of them as reminders—reprinted by permission from the International Mountain Bicycling Association. The basic idea is to prevent or minimize damage to land, water, plants, and wildlife, and to avoid conflicts with other backcountry visitors and trail users. Ride with respect.

IMBA Rules of the Trail

Thousands of miles of dirt trails have been closed to mountain bicyclists. The irresponsible riding habits of a few riders have been a factor. Do your part to maintain trail access by observing the following rules of the trail, formulated by the International Mountain Bicycling Association (IMBA). IMBA's mission is to promote environmentally sound and socially responsible mountain biking.

1. Ride on open trails only. Respect trail and road closures (ask if not sure), avoid possible trespass on private land, obtain permits and authorization as may be required. Federal and state wilderness areas are closed to cycling. The way you ride will influence trail management decisions and policies.

2. Leave no trace. Be sensitive to the dirt beneath you. Even on open (legal) trails, you should not ride under conditions where you will leave evidence of your passing, such as on certain soils after a rain. Recognize different types of soil and trail

MULTIPLE USE TRAIL GUIDELINES

TRAIL COURTESY

YIELD TO

construction; practice low-impact cycling. This also means staying on existing trails and not creating any new ones. Be sure to pack out at least as much as you pack in.

3. Control your bicycle! Inattention for even a second can cause problems. Obey all bicycle speed regulations and recommendations.

4. Always yield trail. Make known your approach well in advance. A friendly greeting (or bell) is considerate and works well; don't startle others. Show your respect when passing by slowing to a walking pace or stopping. Anticipate other trail users at corners and blind spots.

5. Never spook animals. All animals are startled by an unannounced approach, a sudden movement, or a loud noise. This can be dangerous for you, others, and the animals. Give animals extra room and time to adjust to you. When passing horses use special care and follow directions from the horseback riders (dismount and ask if uncertain). Running cattle and disturbing wildlife is a serious offense. Leave gates as you found them, or as marked.

6. Plan ahead. Know your equipment, your ability, and the area in which you are riding—and prepare accordingly. Be self-sufficient at all times, keep your equipment in good repair, and carry necessary supplies for changes in weather or other conditions. A well-executed trip is a satisfaction to you and not a burden or offense to others. Always wear a helmet.

Keep trails open by setting a good example of environmentally sound and socially responsible off-road cycling.

How to Use this Guide

This book describes 39 mountain bike rides in their entirety. A handful of other local routes are mentioned briefly in Appendix A.

Twenty-six of the featured rides are loops, beginning and ending at the same point but coming and going on different trails. Loops are by far the most popular type of ride, and Bozemanites are lucky to have so many so close to home.

Be forewarned, however: the difficulty of a loop ride may change dramatically depending on which direction you ride around the loop. If you are unfamiliar with the rides in this book, try them first as described here. The directions follow the path of least resistance (which does not necessarily mean easy). After you've been over the terrain, you can determine whether a given loop would be fun—or even feasible—in the reverse direction.

Portions of some rides follow gravel or paved roads, and a handful of rides never wander off-road. Purists may wince at road rides in a book about mountain biking, but these are special rides. They offer a chance to enjoy mountain scenery and fresh air while covering easier, non-technical terrain for people new to the sport. They can also be used by hard-core riders on "active rest" days or when higher elevation trails are closed by mud or snow.

Each ride description in this book follows the same format:

Number and name of the ride: Rides are cross referenced by number throughout this book. In many cases, parts of rides or entire routes can be linked to other rides for longer trips or variations on a standard route. These opportunities are noted, followed by "see Ride(s) #."

For the names of rides I relied on official names of trails, roads, and natural features as shown on national forest and U.S. Geological Survey maps. In some cases deference was given to long-term local custom, as in "Sourdough Creek," which is labeled as Bozeman Creek on some maps and more recent signs.

Location: The general whereabouts of the ride; distance and direction from Bozeman.

Distance: The length of the ride in miles, given as a loop, one way, or round trip.

Time: An estimate of how long it takes to complete the ride, for example: 1 to 2 hours. *The time listed is the actual riding time and does not include rest stops.* Strong, skilled riders may be able to do a given ride in less than the estimated time, while other riders may take considerably longer. Also bear in mind that severe weather, changes in trail conditions, or mechanical problems may prolong a ride.

Tread: The type of road or trail: paved road, gravel road, dirt road or jeep track, doubletrack, ATV-width singletrack, and singletrack.

Aerobic level: The level of physical effort required to complete the ride: easy, moderate, or strenuous. (See the explanation of the rating systems on page 12).

Technical difficulty: The level of bike handling skills needed to complete the ride upright and in one piece. Technical difficulty is rated on a scale from 1 to 5, with 1 being the easiest and 5 the hardest (see the explanation of the rating systems on page 14).

Hazards: A list of dangers that may be encountered on a ride, including traffic, weather, trail obstacles and conditions, risky stream crossings, obscure trails, and other perils. Remember: conditions may change at any time. Be alert for storms, new fences, downfall, missing trail signs, and mechanical failure. Fatigue, heat, cold, and/or dehydration may impair judgment. Always wear a helmet and other safety equipment. Ride in control at all times.

Highlights: Special features or qualities that make a ride worth doing (as if we needed an excuse!): scenery, fun singletrack, chances to see wildlife.

Land status: A list of managing agencies or land owners. Most of the rides in this book are on the Gallatin National Forest. But many of the rides also cross portions of private, state, or municipal lands. Always leave gates as you found them. And respect the land, regardless of who owns it. See Appendix B for a list of local addresses for land-managing agencies.

Maps: A list of available maps. The Gallatin National Forest visitors' map (scaled at 1:126,720) affords a good overview of travel routes in the region. USGS topographic maps in the 7.5-minute quad series provide a close-up look at terrain. Also, the Bureau of Land Management 1:100,000 maps for Ennis and Bozeman show topography and many travel routes for the mountains south of Bozeman. Not all routes are shown on official maps.

Access: How to find the trailhead or the start of the ride. A number of rides can be pedaled right from town; for others it's best to drive to the trailhead.

The ride: A mile-by-mile list of key points—landmarks, notable climbs and descents, stream crossings, obstacles, hazards, major turns and junctions—along the ride. All distances were measured to the tenth of a mile with a cyclo-computer (a bike-mounted odometer). Terrain, riding technique, and even tire pressure can affect odometer readings, so treat all mileages as estimates.

Finally, one last reminder that the real world is changing all the time. The information presented here is as accurate and up-to-date as possible, but there are no guarantees out in the mountains. You alone are responsible for your safety and for the choices you make on the trail.

If you do find an error or omission in this book, or a new and noteworthy change in the field, I'd like to hear from you. Please write to Will Harmon, c/o Falcon Press Publishing, P.O. Box 1718, Helena, MT 59624.

Rating the Rides - One Person's Pain is Another's Pleasure

One of the first lessons learned by most mountain bikers is to not trust their friends' accounts of how easy or difficult a given ride may be.

"Where ya wanna ride today?"

"Let's do 'The Wall' dudes—it's gnarly in the middle, but even my grandma could fly up that last hill, and the view is way cool."

If you don't read between the lines, only painful experience will tell you that granny won the pro-elite class in last weekend's hillclimb race and "the view" is over the handlebars from the lip of a thousand-foot drop on that fun little gnarly stretch.

So how do you know what you're getting into, before it's too late?

Don't always listen to your friends.

But do read this book. *Fat Trax* guides rate each ride for two types of difficulty: the *physical effort* required to pedal the distance, and the level of *bike-handling skills* needed to stay upright and make it home in one piece. We call these **Aerobic level** and **Technical difficulty.**

The following sections explain what the various ratings mean in plain, specific language. An elevation profile accompanies each ride description to help you determine how easy or hard the ride is (see page 13). Also weigh other factors such as elevation above sea level, total trip distance, weather and wind, and current trail conditions.

Aerobic Level Ratings

Bicycling is often touted as a relaxing, low-impact, relatively easy way to burn excess calories and maintain a healthy heart and lungs. Mountain biking, however, tends to pack a little more work (and excitement) into the routine.

Fat tires and soft or rough trails increase the rolling resistance, so it takes more effort to push those wheels around. Unpaved and off-road hills tend to be steeper than grades measured and tarred by the highway department. When we use the word *steep*, we mean a sweat-inducing, oxygen-sucking, lactose-building climb. If it's followed by an exclamation point—steep (!)—expect some honest pain on the way up (and maybe for days afterward).

So expect to breathe hard and sweat some, probably a lot. Pedaling around town is a good start, but it won't fully prepare you for the workout offered by most of the rides in this book. If you're unsure of your level of fitness, see a doctor for a physical exam before tackling any of the rides in this book. And if you're riding to get back in shape or just for the fun of it, take it easy. Walk or rest if need be. Start with short rides and add on miles gradually.

Here's how we rate the exertion level for terrain covered in this book:

Easy: Flat or gently rolling terrain. No steeps or prolonged climbs.

Moderate: Some hills. Climbs may be short and fairly steep or long and gradual.

Strenuous: Frequent or prolonged climbs steep enough to require riding in the lowest gear; requires a high level of aerobic fitness, power, and endurance (typically acquired through many hours of riding and proper training). Less fit riders may need to walk.

Many rides are mostly easy and moderate but may have short strenuous sections. Other rides are mostly strenuous and should be attempted only after a complete medical checkup and implant of a second heart, preferably a *big* one. Also be aware that flailing through a highly technical section can be exhausting even on the flats. Good riding skills and a relaxed stance on the bike save energy.

Finally, any ride can be strenuous if you ride it hard and fast. Conversely, the pain of a lung-burning climb grows easier to tolerate as your fitness level improves. Learn to pace yourself and remember to schedule easy rides and rest days into your calendar.

Elevation Graphs

An elevation profile accompanies each ride description. Here the ups and downs of the route are graphed on a grid of elevation (in feet above sea level) on the left and miles pedaled across the bottom. Route surface conditions (see map legend), and technical levels are shown on the graphs.

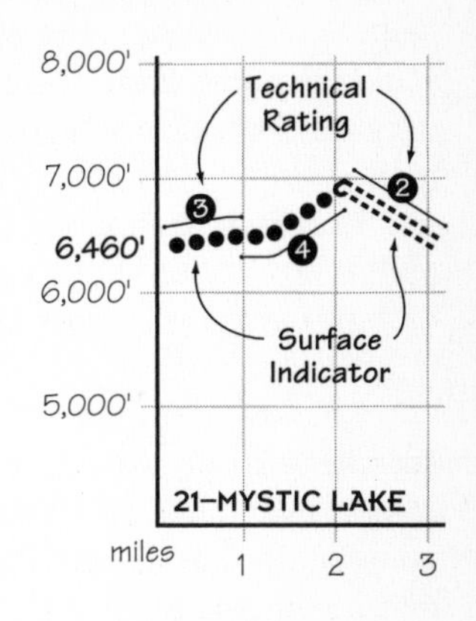

Note that these graphs are compressed (squeezed) to fit on the page. The actual slopes you will ride are not as steep as the lines drawn on the graphs (it just feels that way). Also, some extremely short dips and climbs are too small to show up on the graphs. All such abrupt changes in gradient are, however, mentioned in the mile-by-mile ride description.

Technical Difficulty Ratings

While you're pushing up that steep, strenuous slope, wondering how much farther you can go before your lungs prolapse and billow out of your mouth like an air bag in a desperate gasp for oxygen, remember that the dry heaves aren't the only hurdle on the way to the top of the mountain.

There's that tree across the trail, or the sideslope full of ball-bearing sized pebbles, or the place where the trail disappears except for faint bits of rubber clinging to the smooth, sheer wall of granite straight ahead.

Mountain bikes will roll over or through an amazing array of life's little challenges, but sometimes we, as riders, have to help. Or at least close our eyes and hang on. As a last resort, some riders get off their bikes and walk—get this—*before* they flip over the handlebars. These folks have no sense of adventure.

The rest of us hop onto our bikes with only the dimmest inkling of what lies ahead. Later we brag about the Ride to Hell (leaving out the part about carrying our bikes over hell's highly technical terrain).

No more. The technical difficulty ratings in this book help take the worst surprises out of backcountry rides. In the privacy of your own home you can make an honest appraisal of your bike-handling skills and then find rides in these pages that match your ability.

We rate technical difficulty on a scale from 1 to 5 (1 being easiest). We tried to make the ratings as objective as possible by considering the type and frequency of the ride's obstacles. The same standards were applied consistently through all the rides in this book.

We've also added plus (+) and minus (-) symbols to cover gray areas between given levels of difficulty: a 4+ obstacle is harder than a 4, but easier than a -5. A stretch of trail rated as 5+ would be unrideable by all but the most skilled (or luckiest) riders.

Here are the 5 levels defined:

Level 1: Smooth tread; road or doubletrack; no obstacles, ruts, or steeps. Requires basic bike riding skills.

Level 2: Mostly smooth tread; wide, well-groomed singletrack or road/doubletrack with minor ruts or loose gravel or sand.

Level 3: Irregular tread with some rough sections; single or doubletrack with obvious route choices; some steep sections; occasional obstacles may include small rocks, roots, water bars, ruts, loose gravel or sand, and sharp turns or broad, open switchbacks.

Level 4: Rough tread with few smooth places; singletrack or rough doubletrack with limited route choices; steep sections, some with obstacles; obstacles are numerous and varied, including rocks, roots, branches, ruts, sidehills, narrow tread, loose gravel or sand, and switchbacks.

Level 5: Continuously broken, rocky, root-infested, or trenched tread; singletrack or extremely rough doubletrack with few route choices; frequent, sudden, and severe changes in gradient; some slopes so steep that wheels lift off ground; obstacles are nearly continuous and may include boulders, logs, water, large holes, deep ruts, ledges, piles of loose gravel, steep sidehills, encroaching trees, and tight switchbacks.

Again, most of the rides in this book cover varied terrain, with an ever-changing degree of technical difficulty. Some trails run smooth with only occasional obstacles, and other trails are seemingly all obstacle. The path of least resistance, or *line*, is where you find it. In general, most obstacles are more challenging if you encounter them while climbing than while descending. On the other hand, in heavy surf (e.g., boulder fields, tangles of downfall, cliffs), fear plays a larger role when facing downhill.

Realize, too, that different riders have different strengths and weaknesses. Some folks can scramble over logs and boulders without a grunt, but they crash head over heels on every switchback turn. Some fly off the steepest drops and others freeze. Some riders climb like the wind and others just blow...and walk.

The key to overcoming "technical difficulties" is practice: keep trying. Follow a rider who makes it look easy, and don't hesitate to ask for constructive criticism. Try shifting your weight (good riders move a lot, front to back, side to side, and up and down) and experimenting with balance and momentum. Find a smooth patch of lawn and practice riding as slowly as possible, even balancing at a standstill in a "track stand" (described in the Glossary). This will give you more confidence—and more time to recover or bail out—the next time the trail rears up and bites.

The Name Game

Mountain bikers often assign their own descriptive nicknames to trails—"Nick's Nightmare," "Top Speed," and "Catastrophe" all pertain to Bozeman-area rides.

These nicknames may help to distinguish or describe certain parts of the overall ride, but only for the group of people that knows the nickname. All too often the nicknames are meaningless—or misleading—to cyclists who haven't spun their pedals on the weekly Wednesday evening group ride.

A case in point is the "Wall of Death," familiar to most of us as Forest Service Trail 436 to Mystic Lake. In places the trail narrows and runs across steep sideslopes. It's not for beginners or folks with an extreme fear of falling. But neither is it a "wall," and to date no sprocket rocketeer has died on this stretch of trail. Unfortunately, the name alone scares some riders away.

Geez, that sounds like a truth-in-advertising sermon. Don't get me wrong—trail nicknames can be clever, descriptive, even helpful. (Some of my favorites from around the state include "Star Wars," where the trailside trees blur at high speed like the stars in *Return of the Jedi* when the Millennium Falcon goes into hyperspace; "Strip Search," which vanishes in a thicket of alder where branches grope, poke, and rip at Lycra from all directions; and "Youth in Asia," a veiled reference to the only cure for a terminal climb.)

But for the sake of clarity, I stuck to the official (or at least most widely accepted) names for the trails and roads described in this book. Where a route is commonly known by more than one name, the other names are mentioned. If you know them by some other name, or if you come up with nicknames that peg the personalities of these rides, then by all means share them with your riding buddies.

A Short Index of Rides

Road Rides

(includes jeep tracks and unmaintained routes)

4. Story Hills Radio Tower Hillclimb
5. Kelly Canyon Loop
6. West Bridger Foothills Road Loop
10. Flathead Pass Hillclimb
12. Petterson Road
17. Skunk Creek Loop
20. Sourdough Creek (road option)
24. Lower Hyalite-Sourdough Loop
35. Upper Squaw Creek Road
39. Missouri Headwaters Loop

Sweet Singletrack Rides

(may also include road and doubletrack portions)

1. Sourdough Ridge Loop (1 to 3)
3. Sourdough Creek Nature Trail (1 to 3)
7. Sypes Canyon (3 to 5+)
9. Truman Gulch (3 to 4+)
13. Shafthouse Loop (3 to 5+)
14. Fairy Lake-Brackett Creek Loop (2 to 4)
15. Ross Pass Loop (2 to 4)

16. Grassy Mountain Loop (1 to 4+)
18. Stone Creek Loop (2 to 4)
19. Olson-Stone Loop (1 to 4+)
20. Sourdough Creek (trail option) (2 to 4)
22. Leverich Canyon A Loop (1 to 4)
23. Leverich Canyon B Loop (1 to 4)
25. Moser Creek Loop (2 to 3)
26. History Rock Loop (1 to 3+)
27. Hyalite Reservoir Loop (1 to 3+)
28. Lick Creek-Hood Creek Loop (1 to 4)
31. Emerald Lake (3+ to 5)
32. Garnet Mountain Loop (2 to 4)
34. Mica Creek Loop (2 to 3)
38. Flattop Mountain (3 to 4+)

Beginner's Luck

1. Sourdough Ridge Loop (1 to 3)
2. Gallagator Trail (2)
3. Sourdough Creek Nature Trail (1 to 3)
4. Story Hills Radio Tower Hillclimb (1 to 3)
24. Lower Hyalite-Sourdough Loop (1 to 2)
30. Grotto Falls (1)
35. Upper Squaw Creek Road (2)

Technical Tests

8. Middle Fork of Cottonwood Canyon (5+)
21. Mystic Lake Loop (4 to 5)
31. Emerald Lake (3 to 4+)
36. Swan Creek Loop (4 to 5+)

Great Climbs—the Yearn to Burn

7. Sypes Canyon
10. Flathead Pass Hillclimb
13. Shafthouse Loop
15. Ross Pass Loop
16. Grassy Mountain Loop
18. Stone Creek Loop
26. History Rock Loop
31. Emerald Lake
32. Garnet Mountain
38. Flattop Mountain

Great Downhills—the Need for Speed

7. Sypes Canyon
9. Truman Gulch
13. Shafthouse Loop
15. Ross Pass Loop
16. Grassy Mountain Loop
17. Skunk Creek Loop
18. Stone Creek Loop
20. Sourdough Creek Loop
22. Leverich Canyon A Loop
23. Leverich Canyon B Loop
24. Lower Hyalite-Sourdough Loop
25. Moser Creek Loop
26. History Rock Loop
31. Emerald Lake
34. Mica Creek Loop
37. Little Bear to Swan Creek
38. Flattop Mountain

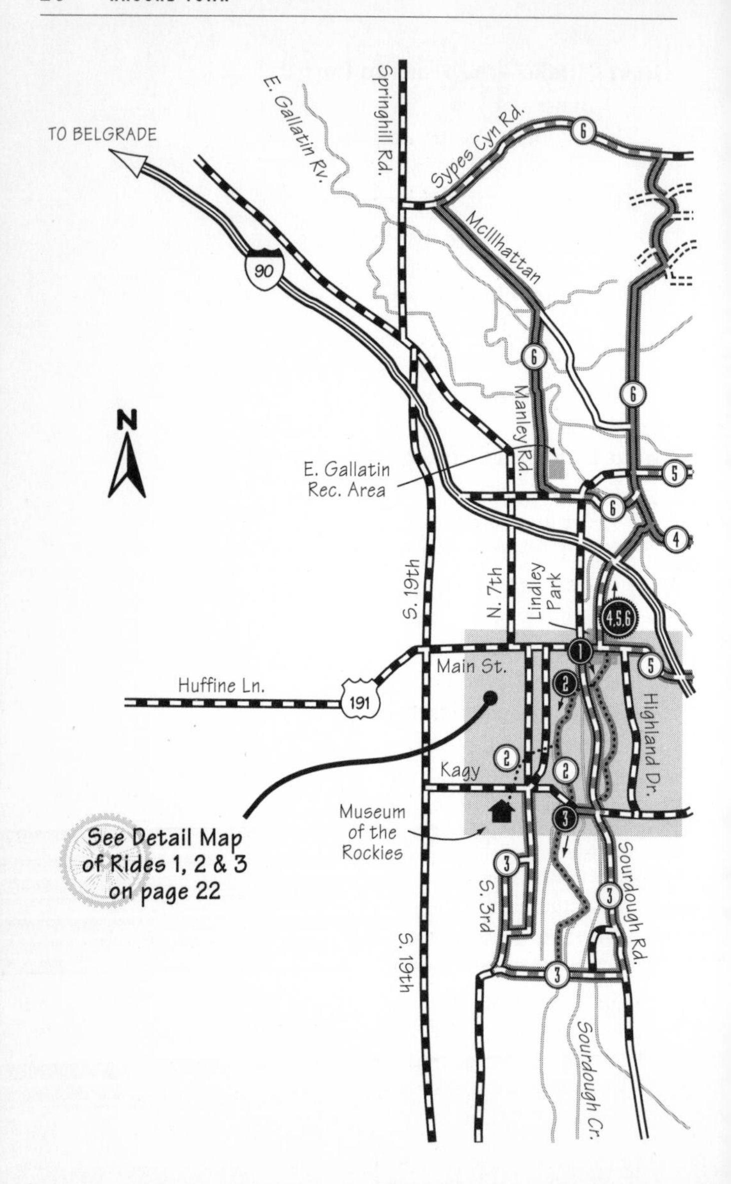
TO BELGRADE
E. Gallatin Rv.
Springhill Rd.
Sypes Cyn Rd.
McIlhattan
90
N
E. Gallatin
Rec. Area
Manley Rd.
S. 19th
N. 7th
Lindley
Park
4,5,6
Main St.
Huffine Ln.
191
Highland Dr.
Kagy
Museum
of the
Rockies
See Detail Map
of Rides 1, 2 & 3
on page 22
S. 3rd
Sourdough Rd.
S. 19th
Sourdough Cr.

AROUND TOWN
Rides 1, 2, 3, 4, 5, 6

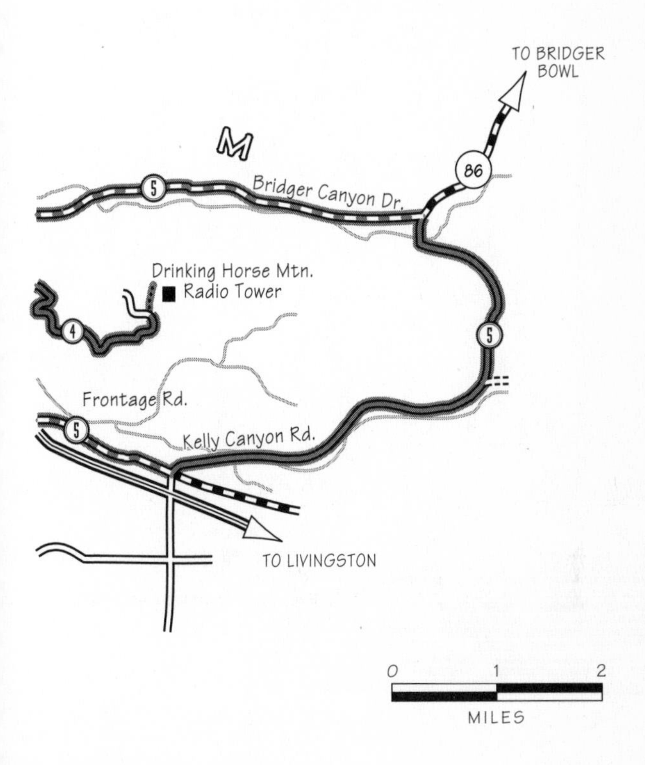

DETAIL MAP AROUND TOWN

Rides 1, 2, 3

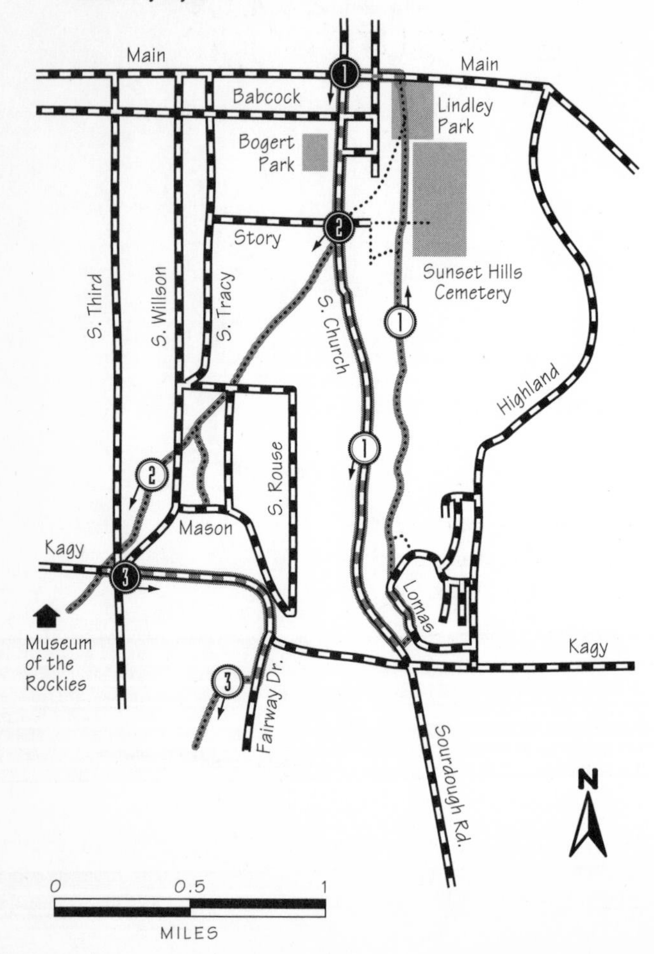

Sourdough Ridge Loop

Location: On the east edge of Bozeman's city limits.

Distance: 3.5-mile loop.

Time: 40 minutes to 1 hour.

Tread: 1.6 miles on paved road; 1.9 miles on singletrack or gravel path.

Aerobic level: Mostly easy, with two short but strenuous climbs.

Technical difficulty: 1 on roads, 3 on singletrack.

Hazards: Watch for traffic on South Church/Sourdough Road; yield to other trail users; Burke Park path is loose gravel—slow down for other trail users and when turning.

Highlights: Fine, swoopy singletrack right in town; good views of town and the Gallatin Valley; scintillating sunsets.

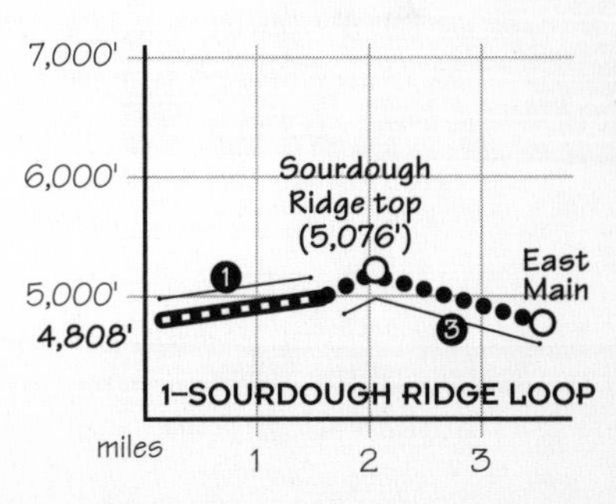

Land status: Private; City of Bozeman.

Maps: Bozeman Chamber of Commerce city map; USGS Bozeman.

Access: The entire loop is in Bozeman city limits and can be accessed from many points along its route. We'll start at the corner of South Third and East Main streets. Visitors can park and picnic at Bogert Park, 3 blocks south of Main on South Third.

The ride:

0.0 From the corner of South Church and East Main pedal south on South Church, which becomes Sourdough Road as it leaves town.

0.2 (3 blocks) Bogert Park. A good post-ride place to relax. Swimming pool, playground, picnic pavilion.

0.4 Corner of South Church and Story Street. Note Pete's Hill on the left; the trails here are one option for ending this loop ride. Pedal south on South Church; watch for traffic on this narrow winding road.

1.6 Watch for a pair of pullouts on the left (east) side of the road. Turn into the second (smaller) one, about 100 feet before the intersection with Kagy Boulevard. The singletrack return to town begins here. Gear down for the steep 50-foot climb through the weed patch and stay on the trail—this is private property.

1.7 Roll down to the pavement and turn left onto Lomas Drive. Pedal 70 yards to the corner of Lomas and O'Connell and go straight (north) back into the weeds, gearing down again for the strenuous singletrack climb onto Sourdough Ridge. After about 50 yards of climbing the trail forks. Right goes to the top of a low knob and the upper neighborhood. Bear left to stay on singletrack that rolls in and out of swales along the west face of the ridge.

2.1 Burke Park gate and sign (5,076 feet). Go through the

gate and turn left onto dirt singletrack. (Or stay straight on the wide gravel path; both routes end up in the same place.) The braided singletrack follows the contours of the ridge west of the gravel park path, sometimes re-joining it for short distances.

2.7 Two wooden posts on the gravel path mark twin singletracks dropping left to Pete's Hill. Pick a track, or stay on the gravel if other trail users are on the singletrack.

2.9 Pete's Hill. Turn left down a set of 4+ switchbacks or drop straight down along the fenceline for the shortest route back to town. For one last burst of singletrack, veer right at the fence and pass through the opening. The gravel path goes right into Sunset Hills Cemetery; instead go straight on the wide dirt singletrack. CAUTION: Watch for other trail users on this overgrown trail. Bank right and uphill to stay on the main track and then release the brakes (if the trail ahead is clear) for a swoopy downhill on singletrack through the lawns of Lindley Park. Skirt a pond on the left and cross the culvert.

3.5 East Main, about one block east of South Church.

Variation: Riders who want to avoid singletrack can still enjoy Sourdough Ridge. Follow the route described above to mile 1.6. Then use these directions:

1.6 Turn left onto Kagy Boulevard and pedal east up the moderate hill.

1.8 Turn left onto Highland and pedal north.

2.0 Turn left onto Berthot, then right on Baxter, then left on O'Connell, and finally right on Kenyon. A sign warns: "Road Closed except local property owners 8 p.m. to 6 a.m." Pedal uphill on Kenyon.

2.2 Top of knob (see mile 1.7 in singletrack version). Lean right to stay on pavement.

2.3 Pavement ends; pedal north on dirt doubletrack to Burke Park. From here, follow the wide gravel path north to Sunset Hills Cemetery and the access road through Lindley Park (see description above).

3.6 East Main.

Gallagator Trail

Location: In Bozeman, running southwest from South Church to the Museum of the Rockies on Kagy Boulevard. ***See map on page 22.***

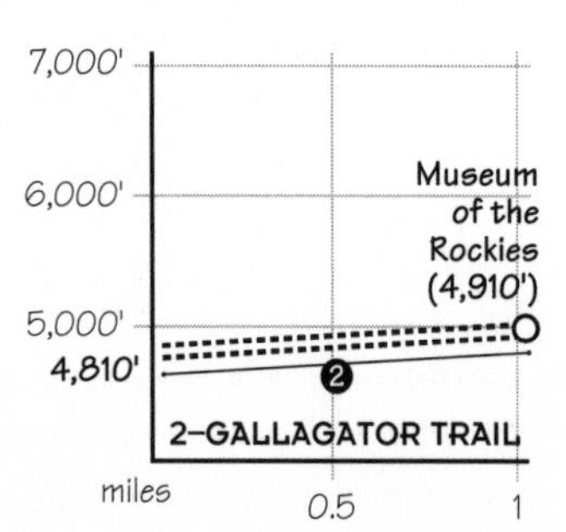

Distance: 1.1 miles one way.

Time: About 10 minutes.

Tread: Wide gravel path on old railroad bed.

Aerobic level: Easy.

Technical difficulty: 2 (some curb hopping).

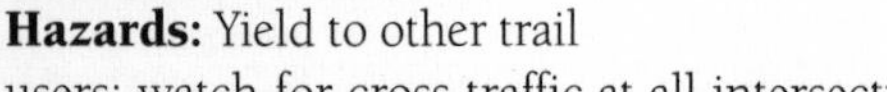

Hazards: Yield to other trail users; watch for cross traffic at all intersections, especially on South Church, Garfield, Willson, Third, and Kagy.

Highlights: An easy, off-road family ride in town; duck ponds; Museum of the Rockies.

Land status: Private; City of Bozeman; Montana State University.

Maps: Bozeman Chamber of Commerce city map (trail is not shown); USGS Bozeman.

Access: The Gallagator Trail has official access points at the corner of South Church and Story Street, on east Garfield, on South Willson just south of Grant Street, on South Third just north of Kagy Boulevard, and at the Museum of the Rockies. Many other informal paths and openings allow access from neighborhoods on both sides of the trail. Let's start at the corner of Story and South Church and work our way south.

The ride:

0.0 At the corner of Story and South Church (across the road from Pete's Hill—see Ride 1) look 30 feet south on the west side of South Church for several wooden posts and a sign marking the Gallagator Trail. Formerly a railroad track, this wide gravel path runs south-southwest through the backyards of Bozeman's east end neighborhoods. CAUTION: Yield to other trail users. Watch for pedestrians, dogs, and other cyclists, especially where side trails join in.

0.1 Wooden bridge over Sourdough Creek.

0.2 Another wooden bridge.

0.4 Yet another wooden bridge.

0.5 East Garfield Street. Stop at the curb and look both ways for traffic before crossing.

0.6 Trail forks. To stay on the Gallagator Trail, lean uphill and right at the forks. The trail angles between two duck ponds and soon meets South Willson. Or: left drops and winds through Langohr Community Gardens (watch for rabbits and ducks on trail). Riders aiming for the Sourdough Nature Trail (see Ride 3) should go left and follow the trail to Mason Street. Juke left on

Mason to South Tracy and continue south to Kagy Boulevard. Turn left and pedal east 0.2 mile, then turn right onto Fairway Drive. See Ride 3 for further directions.

0.7 South Willson. Pedal south about 60 feet on the sidewalk and cross Willson where the Gallagator takes off on the other side (it's marked again by wooden posts).

0.9 Cross South Third Street; use the curb cut on the other side of Third and continue southwest.

1.0 Hop the curbs and median on Kagy Boulevard. Watch for traffic!

1.1 Trail ends at Museum of the Rockies by a large horse sculpture and several picnic tables.

Sourdough Creek Nature Trail

Location: On the south edge of Bozeman, running south from Kagy Boulevard near the Valley View Gold Club to Goldenstein Road. ***See map on page 22.***

Distance: 4.3-mile loop.

Time: 1 to 2 hours.

Tread: 3.1 miles on paved roads; 1.2 miles on singletrack.

Aerobic level: Easy.

Technical difficulty: 1 on roads; 2 to 3 on singletrack.

Hazards: Yield to other trail users; ride during low-use times; some bridges in poor condition.

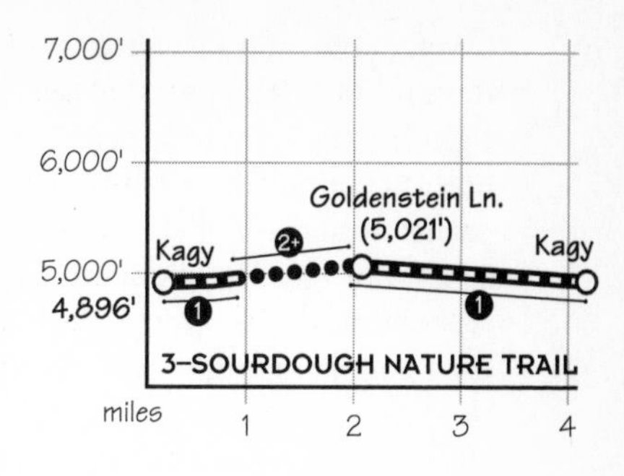

Highlights: An easy off-road ride near town along a beautiful stream, with good opportunities to see wildlife, especially birds.

Land status: Private; City of Bozeman.

Maps: Bozeman Chamber of Commerce city map (trail not shown); USGS Bozeman.

Access: This ride begins and ends on the south edge of Bozeman. Pedal to the intersection of South Willson Avenue and Kagy Boulevard just east of the Museum of the Rockies. (The Gallagator Trail—Ride 2—provides ready access to this ride for residents of Bozeman's southeast side.)

The ride:

0.0 From the corner of South Willson Avenue and Kagy Boulevard pedal east on Kagy. CAUTION: Watch for traffic. The road is signed as a bicycle route; slow-moving riders and family groups may want to ride on the double-wide sidewalk.

0.4 Turn right onto Fairway Drive and pedal south through the upscale neighborhood that lines Valley View Country Club.

0.7 Just past the sign marking Fairway as a private road, turn right, off the pavement at a low wooden fence.

Several posts and a sign mark the beginning of the Sourdough Trail. Pedal west about 30 feet and lean left (a right here goes up to Spring Creek Drive and the neighborhood off of South Third). Follow the winding gravel path south.

1.0 The trail seems to end on West Graf Street. Turn left and ride the sidewalk, crossing Spring Meadow Drive, and turn left again where a ranch-style gate and sign span the Sourdough Trail. The trail narrows slightly and slices between the golf course on the left and a row of homes on the right. Then it veers south for the line of poplars and cottonwoods marking Sourdough Creek.

1.3 The trail turns to dirt (can be muddy into early summer and after any rain) and tends to braid in places. Watch for the first stream crossing (as of this writing the wooden bridge is defunct as a bridge but provides excellent cover for trout). The trail dives into the trees (and in and out of a handful of boggy potholes).

1.4 The second bridge is also in the drink from time-to-time. Somebody actually does a good job of repairing these bridges, but flooding and heavy trail traffic make it a recurring problem. Across the creek, the trail forks. Go right (left ends in the Gardner Park subdivision).

1.6 Another bridge, this one stout and well above the water. A sign for the Sourdough Trail and Gardner Park urges visitors to slow down and enjoy the shade and babbling brook. Wise advice for bikers on a busy trail. A well-ridden line down the middle of this groomed gravel section of trail invites speed, but heavy foliage makes every kink in the trail into a blind turn. Please ride in control and yield to all other trail users.

1.9 The trail abruptly breaks out of the trees and onto Goldenstein Lane (5,021 feet). Right leads 0.9 mile to South Third (and another 2.1 miles back to Kagy Boulevard); left leads 0.3 mile to Sourdough Road. For the most pleasant loop back to town, turn left and pedal east on Goldenstein.

2.3 Turn left on Sourdough Road. (A right here leads south to Nash Road and access to trails in the Sourdough Creek Drainage. See rides 20, 21, and 22.)

4.3 Kagy Boulevard. Go straight on Sourdough (with access to the ridge trail; see Ride 1) or left on Kagy to return to town proper.

Story Hills Radio Tower Hillclimb

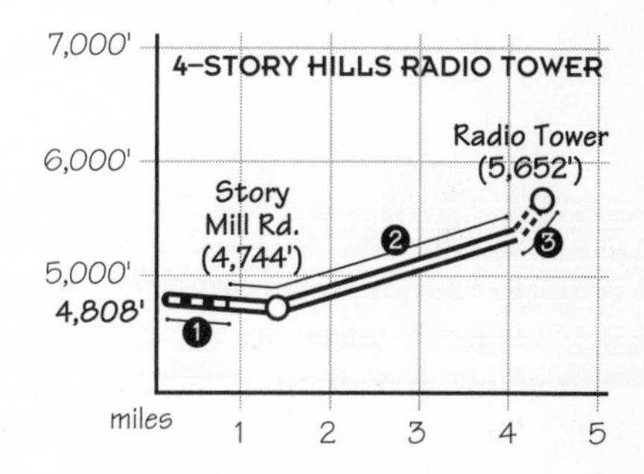

Location: In the grassy foothills on the northeast edge of Bozeman. ***See map on page 20.***

Distance: 4.2 miles one way.

Time: 1 to 2 hours, round trip.

Tread: 0.7 mile on paved road; 3.1 miles on gravel road; 0.4 mile on bumpy doubletrack.

Aerobic level: Easy and moderate; final 0.2 mile of hillclimb is strenuous, gaining 300 feet in elevation.

Technical difficulty: 1 to 2; final hillclimb is 3.

Hazards: Watch for traffic in town; loose gravel (especially on Story Hill Road on descent); high lightning risk during thunderstorms; and a sign near the summit reads: "WARNING: High-level electro-magnetic fields present in this area. ANSI/ OSHA Exposure limits: Adults - 10 minutes, Children - not recommended behind this sign."

Highlights: Best long hillclimb close to town; good early and late-season ride; views of Gallatin Valley and surrounding mountains.

Land status: Private. Sign at entrance reads: "NOTICE: Story Hills is private property. The roads are private! Sightseers are welcome on main road only! No off road traffic by any thing with wheels."

Maps: USGS Bozeman, Kelly Creek.

Access: Begin riding from the corner of East Main and North Wallace in Bozeman (across the street from Heebs Grocery). Or drive to Story Mill Road (see miles 0.0 through 1.3 below), park, and begin riding at the Story Hills entrance.

The ride:

0.0 Corner of North Wallace and East Main; go north on North Wallace.

0.6 Stay on main route as Wallace bends right.

0.7 Pavement ends. Pedal over two railroad crossings and around post-and-pole plant. Wallace becomes L Street as it leaves town.

1.3 Turn right on Story Mill Road and go under Story Hills entrance gate. Begin steady climb on loose gravel road.

3.8 (2.5 miles from entrance gate) turn right on cobbly doubletrack; begin final climb to radio tower. Foot and bike traffic only. The grade steepens near the summit. CAUTION: strong electromagnetic fields may cause health problems (see the warning under "Hazards" above).

4.2 Radio tower; summit (5,652 feet). Return to town along the same route. Back at the entrance gate, heading north on Story Mill Road leads to North Rouse/Bridger Canyon Drive (to extend the ride—see Ride 6—or for a different route back to town).

Kelly Canyon Loop

Location: In the foothills immediately northeast of Bozeman. ***See map on page 20.***

Distance: 15.3-mile loop.

Time: 1.5 to 2 hours.

Tread: 8.5 miles on paved roads; 6.8 miles on gravel roads.

Aerobic level: Mostly easy with a moderate (or strenuous for riders accustomed to paved grades) 0.7-mile climb.

Technical difficulty: 1 and 2.

Hazards: Watch for traffic, especially on Frontage Road and Bridger Canyon Drive (MT 86); loose gravel and washboards on Kelly Canyon Road as it descends into Bridger Canyon.

Highlights: Pastoral, non-technical ride close to town; good year-round ride; views of southern end of the Bridger Range.

Land status: Private.

Maps: USGS Bozeman, Kelly Creek.

Access: Ride from town. Begin at the corner of East Main and Wallace streets in Bozeman.

The ride:

0.0 Pedal east on East Main, climbing the hill past Lindley Park and continuing east out of town. The road drops toward the interstate and doglegs north.

1.0 I-90 interchange. Stay on East Main, which becomes Frontage Road as it leaves town. The road bends east again after passing beneath I-90. CAUTION: Watch for traffic, especially cars entering and exiting the interstate.

2.5 Turn left onto gravel Kelly Canyon Road (signed). The road crosses railroad tracks and forks. Straight is Story Hills Road, which deadends. Instead, lean right to stay on Kelly Canyon Road. This smooth, hardpan road runs straight and level beside the rails and Rocky Creek.

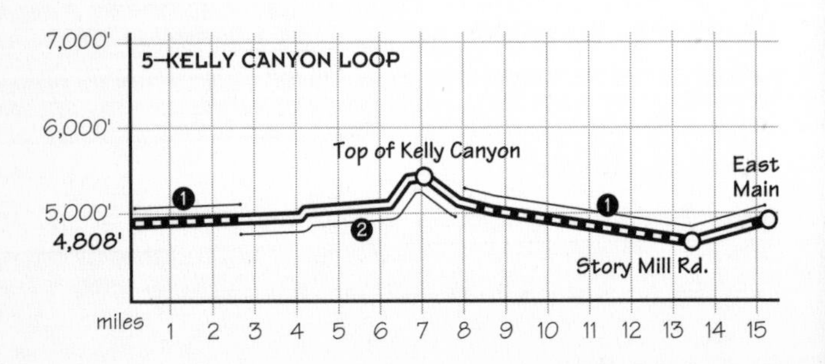

3.1 One-lane bridge over creek.
4.1 The road begins climbing, gently at first, then swings north and into the mouth of Kelly Canyon. The Gallatin Valley may be drowning under tracts of three-bedroom houses, but Kelly Canyon remains farmland, far from the traffic lights and trendy shops of downtown. The grade rolls easily upward, following the meanders of brushy Kelly Creek. Watch for deer in grain fields here (a good excuse for early morning rides).
6.3 Grade eases briefly, then road banks left (north) and begins moderate (strenuous compared to most paved roads in the area) climb.
6.5 Road (actually a private drive) on right; stay straight and continue gasping for air on Kelly Canyon Road.
7.0 Top of climb; Kelly-Bridger divide (5,415 feet). Limited views north along Bridgers. Begin steep descent. The Bridger Canyon side of this road tends to hold thicker pockets of gravel. Also watch for washboards, especially before and in the middle of turns. Ride in control.
7.8 Private drive on right; lean left.
8.2 Pavement begins.
8.3 Brief climb and then a fast drop to a sharp right turn. Cross a one-lane bridge over Bridger Creek.
8.5 Turn left onto Bridger Canyon Drive (MT 86). Watch for traffic, especially during commuting hours and on weekends. Most of this leg is downhill, except for the short climb out of the slide area and past the "M" parking lot.
13.5 Turn left onto gravel Story Mill Road and pedal south past the grain elevators and stockyards.
14.0 Turn right onto L Street (straight here goes into Story Hills; see Ride 4).

14.6 Back onto pavement. The road crosses two railroad tracks and bends south around a post-and-pole yard. L Street becomes North Wallace as it enters town.

15.3 East Main Street.

West Bridger
Foothills Road Loop

Location: On the north edge of Bozeman along the western flank of the Bridger Range. ***See map on page 20.***

Distance: 13.7-mile loop.

Time: 1.5 to 2 hours.

Tread: 5.2 miles on paved road; 8.5 miles on gravel road.

Aerobic level: Easy to moderate.

Technical difficulty: 1 and 2.

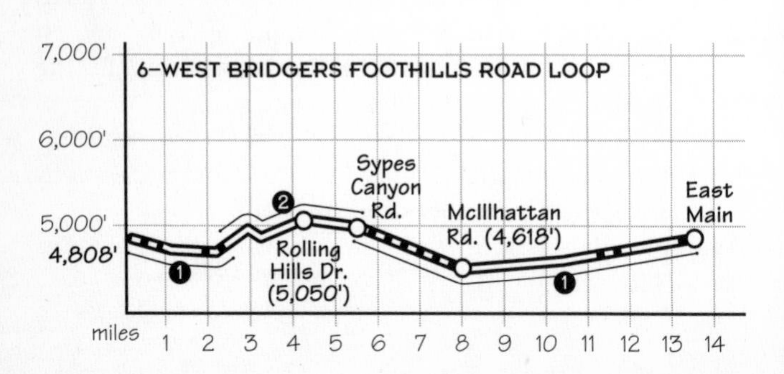

Hazards: Watch for traffic on all roads. Gravel roads may have severe ruts, washboards, and potholes. Cars may kick up dust and stones, especially on McIllhattan and Manley roads.

Highlights: A good early and late-season ride on roads near town that bear little traffic; good views of the south end of the Bridgers and the Gallatin Valley.

Land status: County; private.

Maps: USGS Bozeman.

Access: Begin this loop ride from town on the corner of East Main and North Wallace. The loop begins and ends here and can be ridden in either direction, but the way described here (counterclockwise) affords the most enjoyable downhills.

The ride:

0.0 Corner of North Wallace and East Main; go north on North Wallace.

0.6 Stay on main route as Wallace bends right.

0.7 Pavement ends. Pedal over two railroad crossings and around post-and-pole plant. Wallace becomes L Street as it leaves town.

1.3 Turn left on Story Mill Road and pedal north past the grain elevators and stockyards.

1.8 Bridger Canyon Drive (MT 86). Go straight on Story Mill Road (paved again).

2.2 End of pavement. McIllhattan Road goes left; stay straight and begin moderate climb on rough, rutted Story Mill Road. From here the road rollercoasters (several moderate climbs) through grain fields above Riverside Golf Club and Bozeman's wastewater treatment plant (phew!). This stretch can be impassable after heavy rain.

4.0 Four-way junction. Turn left on Lookfar Lane and climb through a sweeping turn onto a low ridge.
4.1 On top of ridge bear right onto Rolling Hills Drive (5,050 feet); begin long descent through suburbia.
4.4 Bear right (Overlook Lane goes left).
5.2 End of descent.
5.4 Turn left onto paved Sypes Canyon Road and pray the westerlies don't waste a 2.5-mile cruise down smooth macadam.
7.9 Stop sign; turn left onto gravel McIllhattan Road. Pedal southeast on this low bench overlooking the golf course and Bozeman's northern sprawlage.
9.4 Turn right on Manley Road and pedal south.
10.7 Access road to East Gallatin Recreation Area (a reclaimed landfill). Locals call it Bozeman Beach for the sandy shore on one edge of the lake; there are picnic tables and toilets. State officials claim it's safe to swim here.
11.2 Turn left onto paved Griffin Drive.
11.6 Go straight across North Rouse (MT 86) to stay on Griffin Drive.
12.1 Turn right onto gravel Story Mill Road and retrace your tracks.
12.4 Turn right onto L Street which becomes North Wallace in town.
13.7 East Main.

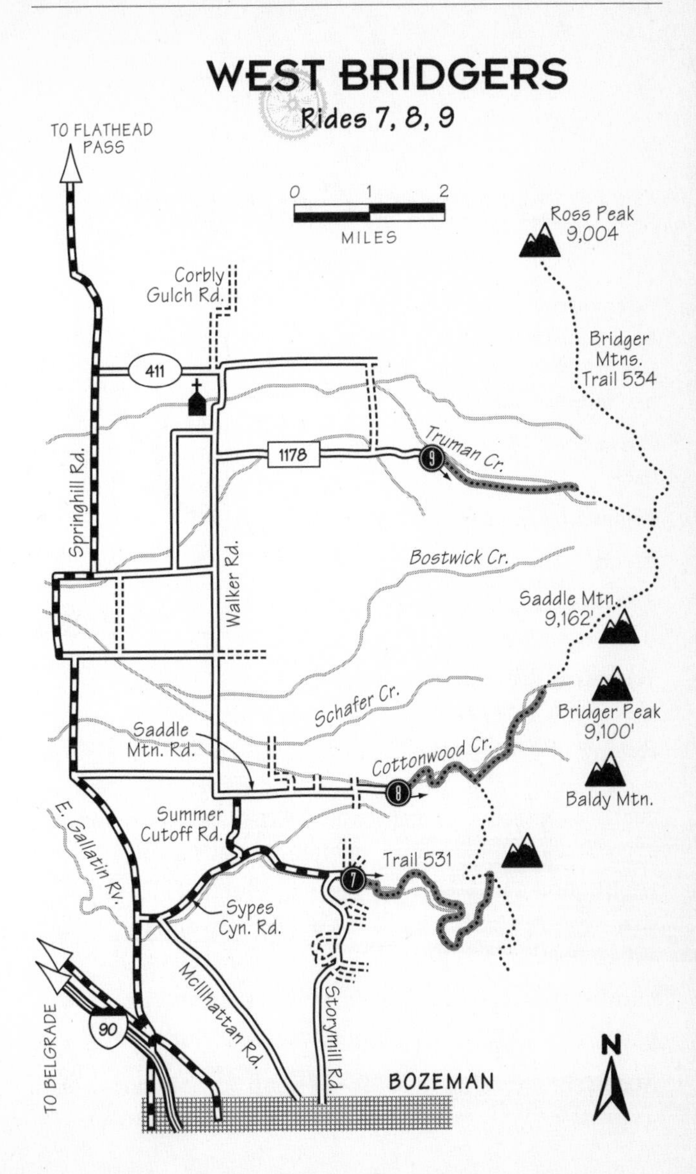
WEST BRIDGERS
Rides 7, 8, 9
TO FLATHEAD PASS
0 1 2
MILES
Ross Peak
9,004
Corbly Gulch Rd.
411
Bridger Mtns. Trail 534
1178
Truman Cr.
Springhill Rd.
Walker Rd.
Bostwick Cr.
Saddle Mtn.
9,162'
Schafer Cr.
Bridger Peak
9,100'
Saddle Mtn. Rd.
Cottonwood Cr.
Baldy Mtn.
Summer Cutoff Rd.
E. Gallatin Rv.
Trail 531
Sypes Cyn. Rd.
McIlhattan Rd.
Storymill Rd.
90
TO BELGRADE
BOZEMAN
N

Sypes Canyon

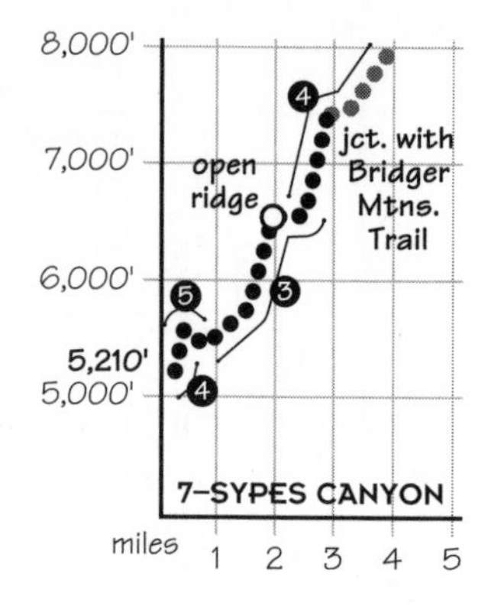

Location: 4 miles north of Bozeman in the southwestern foothills of the Bridger Range. ***See map on page 39.***

Distance: 5.8 miles up and back.

Time: 1 to 2 hours.

Tread: 5.8 miles on singletrack.

Aerobic level: Moderate to strenuous.

Technical difficulty: Mostly 3 and 4 with sections of 5+ near the start.

Hazards: Yield to other trail users and ride in control, especially where trail is overgrown or blind curves limit sight distance. Short section of trail at mile 0.4 traverses an exposed cliff edge. Stay off upper ridge if lightning threatens.

Highlights: Challenging singletrack; a fun hillclimb through shady forest; outstanding views of Bozeman and the Gallatin Valley; wildlife; and possibly the best picnic spot in the area.

Land status: Gallatin National Forest; state; private.

Maps: USGS Kelly Creek, Saddle Peak.

Access: From just north of I-90 on North 7th in Bozeman drive or pedal 0.6 mile east on Griffin Drive. Just after crossing the railroad tracks, turn left onto gravel Manley Road and go 1.8 miles north. Turn left onto McIllhattan Road and go 1.5 miles north to a stop sign. Turn right onto paved Sypes Canyon Road and go 2.7 miles east to the end of the pavement. Continue straight (east) on gravel past a long row of mailboxes and bear right at the fork in front of the first house. Then turn right on Churn Road and go 100 feet to the parking lot and trailhead on the left.

The ride:

0.0 Trailhead for Sypes Canyon Trail 537. Pedal east on the grassy path between the two fencelines. Stay on the designated trail—this is private property.

0.1 Stream crossing; begin moderate climb.

0.2 Steep (!) but short climb—go for it, it's rideable.

0.3 Switchback cuts right and trail climbs strenuously over loose rocks and sand up open hillside.

0.4 Top of initial climb; trail hugs rock outcrop with sheer dropoff on outside edge. Then it drops sharply; several 20-foot sections on talus.

0.5 Resume climb, with a few tough rocky spots.

0.6 Tread becomes mostly smooth and dips in and out of valley bottom, alternating between open south-facing slope (hot in summer) and cool, shadowy forest.

1.1 National forest boundary sign.

1.2 Trail swoops through an abrupt gully.

1.4 Second gully crossing; trail swings onto north-facing side of drainage. Begin 0.5-mile leg through broad switchbacks. Be ready to lunge over some fat water bars.

1.9 Trail spills out on ridge top at a T-junction. Follow trail sign to left.

2.0 Even hardcore trials riders can't resist dabbing here (6,540 feet) to stop and savor the view. Bozeman glimmers to the south and the Gallatin Valley sweeps west to the shadows of the Tobacco Roots on the horizon. This is a great picnic spot (the ever-present breeze discourages flies and mosquitoes) and turn-around point for most folks. Diehards can keep climbing through meadows of arrowleaf balsam root to higher points on the ridge.

2.3 Short set of switchbacks up ridge. These are tighter and grow rockier as you climb, but the views get even better, opening up east and north along the flank of the Bridgers.

2.6 Top of small knob. Trail is 4+ here due to rocks and narrow tread. This is a good turn-around for all riders except those permanently numbed by endorphin overload. If you're determined to keep going, drop across the flat saddle and begin a quad-trashing, 5+ climb.

2.9 Top of big knob. OK, we made it. *Now* can we turn around? Enjoy the descent, but watch your speed and don't run over any hikers, please.

Middle Fork of Cottonwood Canyon

Location: 6 miles north of Bozeman on the western flank of the Bridgers. ***See map on page 39.***

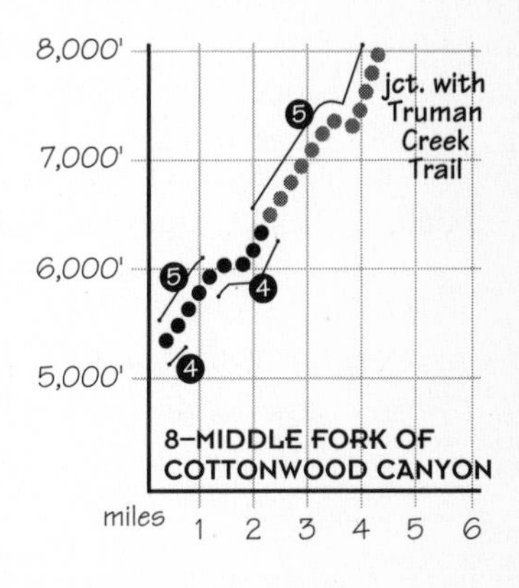

Distance: 4.2 miles up and back, or longer for masochists.

Time: 1.5 to 2 hours, round trip.

Tread: 2 miles of extremely technical singletrack; see it from a new angle on the return ride.

Aerobic level: Easy to moderate, with short strenuous pitches.

Technical difficulty: Mostly 5, with short stretches of 3 and 4.

Hazards: Yield to other trail users. Boulder gardens can trap wheels, feet, elbows, and anything else that wedges between the rocks; falls are likely. Stream crossings may be dangerous during high water or when attempted at high speed.

Highlights: A great test piece for advanced riders; a mini trials course surrounded by rugged mountain scenery.

Land status: Private; Gallatin National Forest.

Maps: Gallatin National Forest; USGS Miser Creek, Saddle Peak.

Access: From just north of I-90 on North 7th in Bozeman drive or pedal 0.6 mile east on Griffin Drive. Just after crossing the railroad tracks, turn left onto gravel Manley Road and go 1.8 miles north. Turn left onto McIllhattan Road and go 1.5 miles north to a stop sign. Turn right onto paved Sypes Canyon Road and go 1.2 miles east. Turn left onto Summer Cutoff Road, which loops onto a low ridge through a residential area. Follow the road 1.2 miles north as it dips, then levels off before ending at gravel Saddle Mountain Road. Turn right here and go 1.6 miles east. Turn left at the T intersection, following signs for the Middle Fork of Cottonwood Canyon, and go 0.2 mile north. Turn right at another Cottonwood Canyon sign onto a one-lane gravel track. CAUTION CYCLISTS: heavy, loose gravel. Go 1.2 miles east to the parking lot and trailhead at road's end.

The ride:

0.0 From the parking lot, pedal between the large boulders on the east end and immediately cross the two-plank wooden bridge over Cottonwood Creek. The trail starts out as a wide, rolling braid of singletracks following an old road bed.

0.3 Abrupt gully across the trail.

0.4 National forest boundary.

0.5 Stream crossing. High runoff may discourage some folks from going any farther. During lower water, intrepid riders may try pedaling across here; others can use the stepping stones and portage their bikes. The trail then hairpins left and begins a 0.6-mile obstacle course over roots, large rocks, and short rises. The grade is moderate or easier, but picking a line through the gnarlies is more than enough to raise your heart rate.

1.1 Junction with Bridger Mountain Trail (sign). Right leads 6 hellish miles south to the M above Bridger Canyon Road. Instead, turn left and continue up along the Middle Fork of Cottonwood Creek.

1.3 Begin moderate to strenuous climb through two switchbacks.

1.4 Top of small toe ridge (6,120 feet) with a good viewpoint of the surrounding drainage. This is a good turnaround point. Or forge ahead and drop back down to a lush meadow at creek level for another 0.7 mile of smoother but still challenging singletrack.

1.7 Stream crossing.

1.9 Stream crossing in a gully.

2.1 More stream crossings, some of them difficult to ride. At this point, most riders will be glad to turn back. Those who thrive on adversity can tackle the heartbreaking, beyond-technical 2.5 mile climb to the divide between Cottonwood and Bostwick canyons climbing north on Trail 534. (The trail climbs one nasty set of switchbacks, then drops down to the head of Bostwick Creek before climbing an even harder grade to the head of Truman Gulch. It tops out at 8,170 feet, but the ground lost and gained in Bostwick Creek adds to the overall climb.) Truly crazed pain addicts can then drop 1.5 miles to the head of Truman Gulch and ride out on Trail 535, looping back to town on Walker Road (see Ride 9). This is NOT recommended for those of us who ride for fun.

Truman Gulch

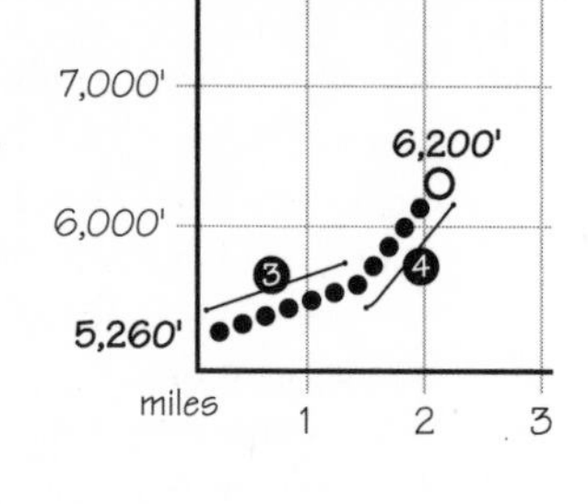

Location: 8 miles north of Bozeman on the west flank of the Bridger Range, immediately southeast of Springhill Community. ***See map on page 39.***

Distance: 4 miles up and back.

Time: 40 minutes to 1.5 hours.

Tread: 2.0 miles of singletrack.

Aerobic level: Moderate.

Technical difficulty: Mostly 3 with sections of 4 to 4+.

Hazards: Yield to other trail users and avoid surprising horseback riders.

Highlights: Cool, shady singletrack with a challenging but eminently rideable line.

Land status: Gallatin National Forest.

Maps: Gallatin National Forest; USGS Miser Creek, Saddle Peak.

Access: From the I-90 overpass on North 7th in Bozeman drive 2.1 miles north on North 7th, which becomes MT 2 as it leaves town. Turn right at the traffic light and drive 8.8 miles north on Springhill Road (County 411). Turn right at the sign for Truman Gulch and Corbly Creek Road and drive 1.7 miles east on

Springhill Community Road. Turn right at Springhill Church onto gravel Walker Road and continue 1.2 miles. Turn left at the sign for Truman Gulch onto FR 1178 and drive 2.2 miles east. At the four-way ranch junction go straight onto the one-lane dirt road. Drive 0.9 mile to the parking lot and trailhead at road's end.

The ride:

0.0 Parking lot and trailhead. Pedal east and around the stock loading ramp to the trail. The trail begins as a wide, smooth track carpeted with pine needles. The upper reaches are rockier and may be slippery. The trail is usually not muddy, but it does stay damp thanks to the dense forest cover.

0.1 Short steep climb.

0.2 Stream crossing.

0.6 Stream crossing.

0.9 Short rocky patch.

1.0 Two stream crossings. Short rocky or rooted sections become more frequent.

1.3 Small side stream crossing.

1.9 Spur trail goes left; stay right. Hardcore riders can attack the short, steep climb; a root step will stop all but the most adroit.

2.0 Small opening and stream crossing (6,200 feet). This is a good turn-around spot. Riders who aren't happy till they're oxygen starved can continue climbing east on the main trail—a level-5, strenuous (!) climb. It rears back and lunges up the valley's north flank and the grade never eases for the next 0.6 mile to the junction with the Bridger Mountains Trail 534 (see also Ride 8).

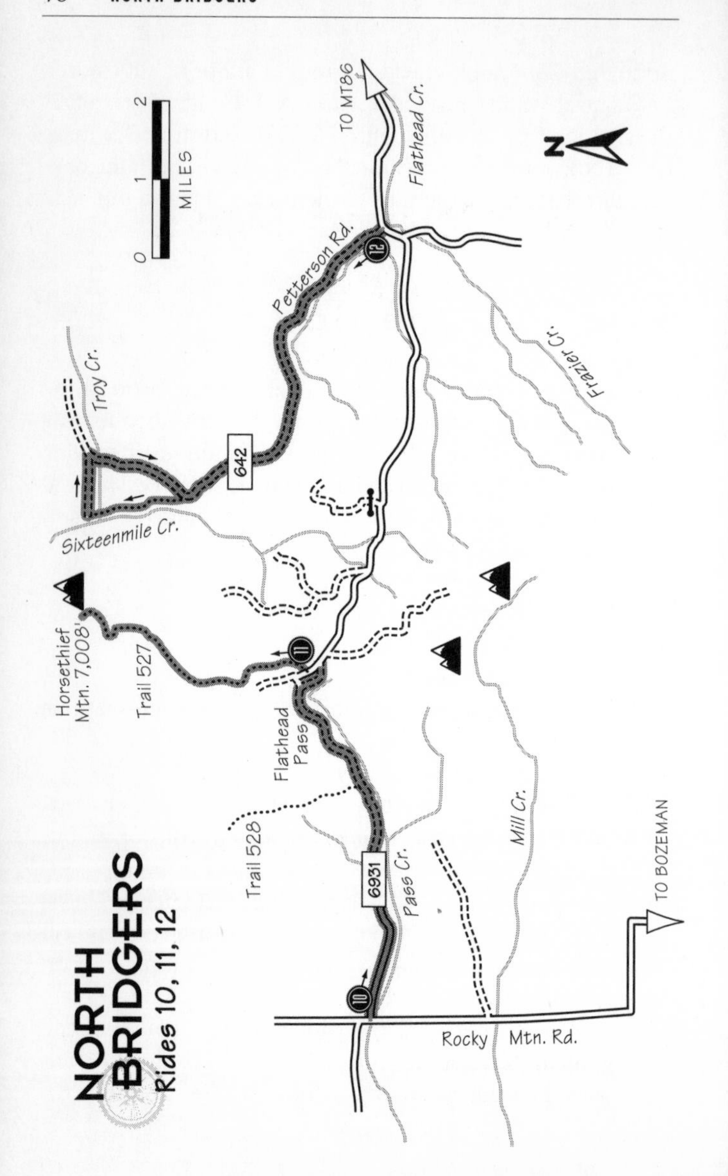
NORTH BRIDGERS
Rides 10, 11, 12
0
1
2
MILES
N
TO MT86
Flathead Cr.
Petterson Rd.
12
Troy Cr.
642
Frazier Cr.
Sixteenmile Cr.
Horsethief Mtn. 7,008'
Trail 527
11
Flathead Pass
Trail 528
6931
Pass Cr.
Mill Cr.
TO BOZEMAN
10
Rocky Mtn. Rd.

Flathead Pass Hillclimb

Location: 21 miles north of Bozeman at the north end of the Bridger Range.

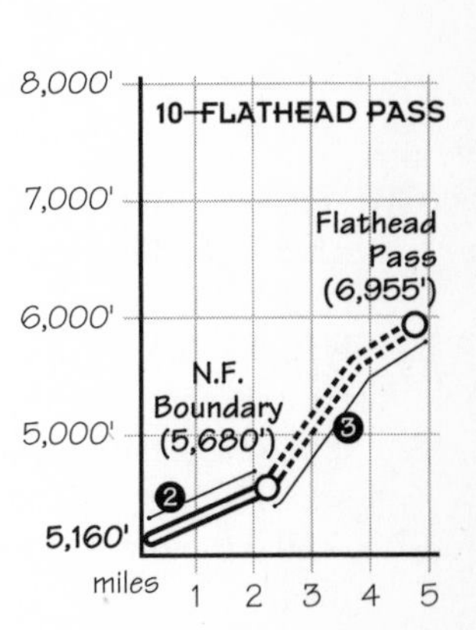

Distance: 4.3 miles one way.

Time: 1 to 2 hours up and back.

Tread: 2.2 miles on gravel road; 2.1 on rough, dirt (often muddy) jeep track.

Aerobic level: Moderate to strenuous.

Technical difficulty: 2 and 3.

Hazards: Some traffic; stay in control on descent.

Highlights: An excellent hillclimb between towering cliffs; good views east and west from atop 6,955-foot Flathead Pass.

Land status: Private; Gallatin National Forest.

Maps: Gallatin National Forest; USGS Flathead Pass.

Access: Since the 1970s a handful of Bozeman diehard bikies have ridden Flathead Pass as a 60-mile loop, pedaling out the west side from town, and then coming back down Bridger Canyon on the east flank of the Bridger Range. It's a marathon of crosswinds, headwinds, hills, and molar-rattling roads.

Try the pass as a 1- to 2-hour fun ride, instead.

From the I-90 overpass on North 7th in Bozeman drive 2.1 miles north on North 7th, which becomes MT 2 as it leaves town. Turn right at the traffic light and drive 11.5 miles north on Springhill Road (County 411). Here the pavement ends and the road doglegs right, then left. It continues north as Rocky Mountain Road; drive another 7.8 miles north to Pass Creek Road on the right (immediately after crossing Pass Creek itself). Park here on the shoulder of the road.

The ride:

0.0 Pedal east on Pass Creek Road, bisecting an old ranch. The road climbs gradually at first, hugging the north bank of Pass Creek.

2.2 National forest boundary; Johnson Canyon off to the right. Beyond here the road becomes a rough jeep track, climbing steadily through a narrowing gorge; expect strong winds, especially in the afternoon.

2.7 Trail 528 climbs away on left; stay straight on main road.

3.2 Road continues climbing between towering gray cliffs; some strenuous sections. Watch for falling rock.

3.7 Jeep track banks left and uphill, climbing hard onto an open, south-facing slope. Follow the track as it rounds this bowl, with a final contour south and east to the pass.

4.3 Flathead Pass (6,955 feet). Look east to the Shields Valley and the Crazy Mountains, and west to the Tobacco Roots. Trail 527 on the flanks of Horse Mountain (Ride 11) takes off to the north of the pass. Return by retracing your tracks downhill.

Horse Mountain
(Trail 527)

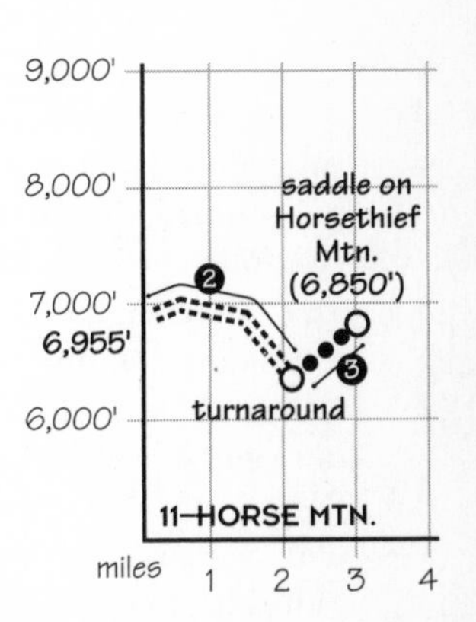

Location: 22 miles north of Bozeman, directly north of Flathead Pass. ***See map on page 48.***

Distance: 2.8 miles out and back (or up to 6 miles round trip for good route-finders).

Time: 30 minutes (much more for extended explorations).

Tread: Grassy (at times muddy) doubletrack on old logging road grade.

Aerobic level: Easy to moderate.

Technical difficulty: 2 to 3.

Hazards: Sudden changes in weather; extreme mud: avoid this route after wet weather and early or late in the year.

Highlights: Views east to the Crazy Mountains; chance to see elk and deer; low visitor use.

Land status: Gallatin National Forest; Big Sky Lumber.

Maps: Gallatin National Forest; USGS Flathead Pass, Hatfield Mountain.

Access: Do this short ride as an extension of the Flathead Pass

Hillclimb (see Ride 10), or as an end in itself. To drive to the trailhead, head north from Bozeman on Bridger Canyon Drive (MT 86). Drive 27 miles north, staying on MT 86, and turn left on Flathead Creek Road (FR 633 then FR 39). Drive west 10.4 miles, staying on the main road, until it tops out on Flathead Pass. Park on the north side of the road in one of several pull-outs.

The ride:

0.0 A rough jeep track scrambles up the ridge going north. Instead, pedal northeast, contouring east of the utility poles and to a gate in the fence. Climb over the gate and continue north on the grassy doubletrack.

0.2 Track enters old clearcut on flank of 8,471-foot Horse Mountain. Continue north.

0.5 Gate and fenceline. Scramble over the gate and climb onto a low saddle (7,000 feet).

0.6 Begin gradual descent toward head of Haw Gulch.

1.4 Old logging road ends; good turn-around point. Determined explorers can continue by cutting uphill and left for 200 yards to unmaintained Trail 527. This rough and hard-to-follow route leads north, rolling 0.6 mile down into the head of Haw Gulch before climbing again to 6,850 feet on the shoulder of Horsethief Mountain. Expect downed trees, a vanishing trail, and steep grades—only experts with map and compass should attempt the leg to Horsethief Mountain. An equally decrepit route breaks off to the left and drops into the head of Quaw Creek, a tributary to the South Fork of Sixteenmile Creek. Both of these trails end on private land north of the Bridgers.

Petterson Road
(FR 642–Middle Fork Road)

Location: 20 miles north of Bozeman on the northeast flank of the Bridger Range. ***See map on page 48.***

Distance: 14 miles.

Time: 2 to 3 hours.

Tread: 10.6 miles on narrow gravel road; 2 miles on jeep track everting to doubletrack; 1.4 miles on singletrack.

Aerobic level: Easy with a few moderate climbs.

Technical difficulty: 1 to 2 on roads; 3 on singletrack.

Hazards: Ruts and mud after wet weather; traffic is light but watch for oncoming vehicles on blind curves.

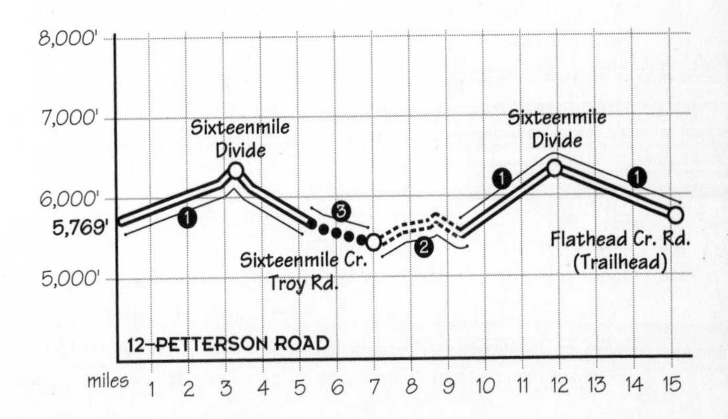

Highlights: A relaxing ride with time to enjoy the scenery and opportunities to see deer and other wildlife. Though the road is open, encountering any traffic is unlikely.

Land status: Private; some Gallatin National Forest.

Maps: Gallatin National Forest; USGS Sedan, Hatfield Mtn.

Access: From Bozeman drive 27 miles north on Bridger Canyon Drive (MT 86). Turn left on Flathead Creek Road (FR 633) and drive west 3.7 miles to Petterson Road (FR 642) on the right. Park on the shoulder of Flathead Creek Road; there's no room at all on Petterson Road.

The ride:

0.0 Pedal northwest onto Petterson Road, climbing briefly above Flathead Creek Road. The road contours easily along a low bench above the Middle Fork of Flathead Creek, offering views west to the north end of the Bridger Range.

1.2 Spur road goes right; bear left and uphill.

1.6 Spur goes right (north). Lean left and climb directly west to the divide between Flathead Creek and the South Fork of Sixteenmile Creek to the north.

3.1 The road swings north and soon begins dropping into the Sixteenmile drainage.

4.3 Trail 522 to Elkhorn Ridge goes right; stay on main road.

4.9 Spur goes left; stay right on the main road as it hugs the creek bank.

5.2 Lean left onto Trail 524. This mostly smooth singletrack runs downstream along the east bank of Sixteenmile Creek, occasionally doglegging around chunks of private property. The Forest Service is in the process of improving sections of the tread and also has plans to better mark the trailhead. Please stay on the trail and watch for horseback riders and other trail users. Also be alert for rattlesnakes.

6.6 Turn right onto the Troy Creek Road doubletrack and begin a moderate climb east and out of the Sixteenmile valley.

7.2 Turn right onto FR 642, here a rough jeep track. Continue climbing to a low ridge with a brief view ahead of the Bridgers. The track drops quickly, juking west to rejoin Sixteenmile Creek at the 524 Trailhead (at mile 5.2 above). Bank left to stay on the main road.

14.0 Flathead Creek Road and your vehicle.

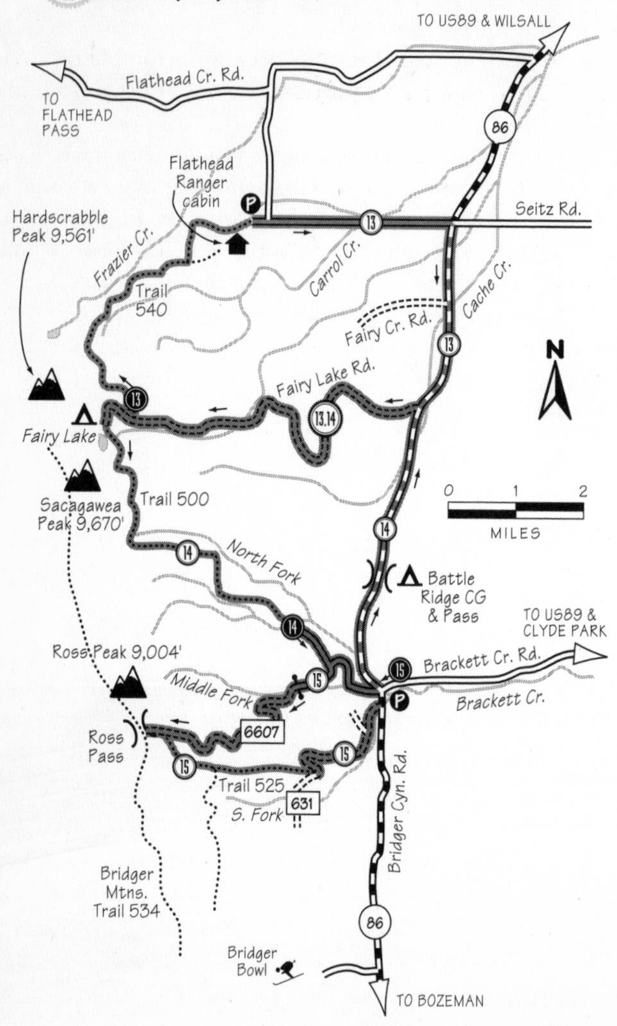

EAST BRIDGERS
Rides 13, 14, 15
TO US89 & WILSALL
TO FLATHEAD PASS
Flathead Cr. Rd.
86
Flathead Ranger cabin
Seitz Rd.
Hardscrabble Peak 9,561'
Frazier Cr.
Carrol Cr.
Trail 540
Cache Cr.
Fairy Cr. Rd.
13
N
Fairy Lake Rd.
13,14
Fairy Lake
Sacagawea Peak 9,670'
Trail 500
0 1 2
MILES
14
North Fork
Battle Ridge CG & Pass
TO US89 & CLYDE PARK
Ross Peak 9,004'
15
Brackett Cr. Rd.
Middle Fork
Brackett Cr.
6607
Ross Pass
Trail 525
631
S. Fork
Bridger Cyn. Rd.
Bridger Mtns. Trail 534
Bridger Bowl
TO BOZEMAN

Shafthouse Loop

Location: 30 miles north of Bozeman on the northeast flank of the Bridger Range.

Distance: 16.8-mile loop.

Time: 2.5 to 4 hours.

Tread: 4.9 miles on singletrack; 5.6 miles on washboarded logging road; 6.3 miles on well-graded gravel road.

Aerobic level: Mostly moderate; 3 miles of strenuous climbing.

Technical difficulty: Mostly 3 to 4, with 0.7 mile of 5+.

Hazards: Watch for traffic on MT 86 and narrow, winding Fairy Lake Road (blind turns); 0.7-mile descent with off-the-seat steeps, small boulders, and trenched singletrack; short stretch of indistinct trail.

Highlights: Spectacular alpine scenery; 4.2 miles of sweet singletrack; good chance of seeing deer, elk, and other wildlife.

Land status: Gallatin National Forest; Big Sky Lumber; private.

Maps: Gallatin National Forest; USGS Sacagawea Peak, Sedan, or Sedan 15-minute quad.

Access: From the corner of Griffin Drive and North Rouse in Bozeman, drive 18 miles north on Bridger Canyon Drive (MT 86) to the three-way intersection at Brackett Creek. Bear left on MT 86 and drive 2.8 miles north, past Battle Ridge Pass and Campground, to Fairy Lake Road. Turn left and drive 5.6 miles west on this winding, one-lane, rugged logging road to a sign marking the Shafthouse trailhead. Park in the small pullout on the left about 70 yards downhill from the sign.

The ride:

0.0 Fairy Lake Road, Shafthouse Trail 540 trailhead. Trail switchbacks up grassy hill to the right of the road. Some steep sections.

0.9 Climb eases; trail winds north toward timberline.

1.2 Top of a broad alpine bench (8,545 feet) with views east to the Crazy Mountains and Shields Valley, south to the Bangtails, and west to Hardscrabble and Sacagawea peaks.

1.5 Begin descent. Follow cairns north down the top of a rounded, grassy shoulder; trail is indistinct.

1.7 Bank right at a cairn and re-enter trees. CAUTION: begin 0.7 mile of technical steep, rocky pitches.

2.4 Trail enters a fir/spruce parkland; gradient eases and tread becomes smoother.

3.3 Trail forks; follow orange blazes left.

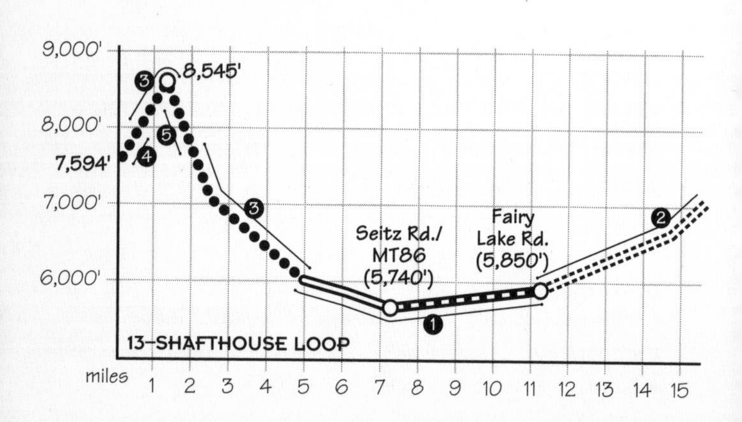

3.9 Fenceline. Trail bends right and follows fence east.
4.3 Barbed-wire gate (please close it behind you). Look west to retrace route and for a great view of the Bridgers.
4.4 100 yards of smooth boardwalk.
4.5 Trail crosses culvert over the North Fork of Carrol Creek; short but steep climb out of ravine.
4.9 Parking lot on 90-degree bend on Flathead Pass Road (FR 6931). Pedal east on FR 6931.
7.4 Junction with MT 86 and Seitz Road. Turn right (south) onto MT 86; watch for traffic.
11.2 Turn right on Fairy Lake Road (and you thought it was steep in your car...).
16.8 Shafthouse trailhead.

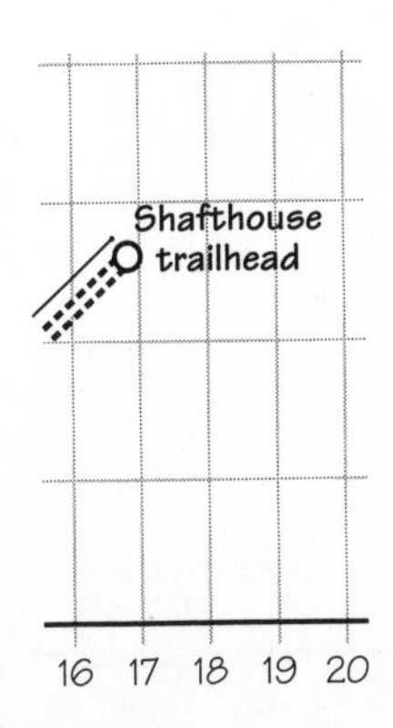

Fairy Lake–Brackett Creek Loop

Location: 30 miles north of Bozeman on the east flank of the Bridger Range. ***See map on page 56.***

Distance: 15.4-mile loop.

Time: 2 to 3 hours.

Tread: 5 miles on singletrack; 7.6 miles on logging road; 2.8 miles on gravel highway.

Aerobic level: Moderate.

Technical difficulty: Mostly 2-3 with short sections of 4.

Hazards: Watch for traffic on MT 86 and Fairy Lake Road; 0.8 mile of slick roots and rocks on climb from Fairy Lake.

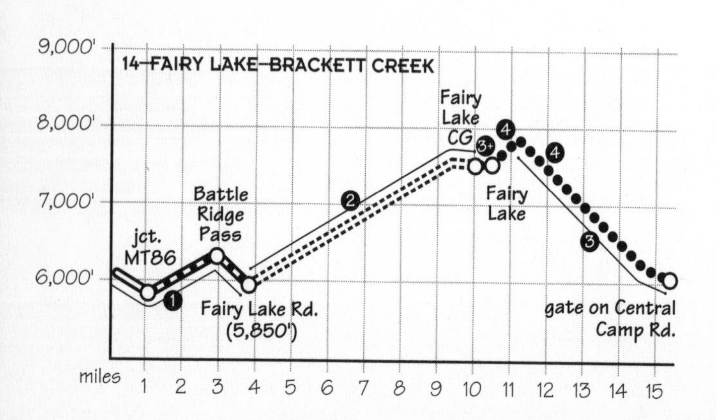

Highlights: Wildflowers, wildlife, and a wild downhill ride. Fairy Lake makes a good (though sometimes crowded) rest stop.

Land status: Gallatin National Forest; private.

Maps: Gallatin National Forest; USGS Sacagawea Peak, Saddle Peak, Grassy Mountain, Sedan.

Access: From the corner of Griffin Drive and North Rouse (MT 86) in Bozeman drive 18 miles north on MT 86 to the end of the pavement at the three-way junction at Brackett Creek. Bear left on MT 86 and turn immediately left onto the Middle Fork Brackett Creek Road (FR 6948). Drive 1 mile west on FR 6948 and turn right onto Central Camp Road (FR 6607). Go about 200 yards to a small parking lot where boulders block the road. Park here and begin by riding back down to MT 86.

The ride:

0.0 Central Camp Road parking lot. Pedal east, back down the Middle Fork Brackett Creek Road.

1.0 Junction with MT 86. Turn left and pedal north on MT 86. The road climbs hard for nearly 2 miles to Battle Ridge Pass and then drops to...

3.8 Fairy Lake Road. Turn left (west) and climb into the Bridgers on this winding, one-lane, bumpy logging road.

10.1 Fairy Lake Campground and day-use parking lot. Take the singletrack that heads south from parking lot and switchbacks down to the lake.

10.2 Fairy Lake; stay on east shore heading south.

10.3 Cross outlet stream and begin climbing south. Roots and rocks in tread are often wet and slippery.

11.1 End of main climb (7,850 feet); trail rolls through forest.

11.7 Enter wet meadow.
11.9 Short boggy section—may be best to dismount and portage bike.
12.0 The Headwall—two crude switchbacks straight down. Ridden only by body-armored adrenaline junkies.
12.2 Stream crossing (it's rideable).
12.3 Begin short climb.
12.4 Trails tops out above Brackett Creek basin. Begin long descent into meadows of cow parsnips and larkspur.
12.9 Junction with old logging road. Turn left to ride doubletrack; stay straight for more (albeit bumpy) singletrack.
13.3 Second junction with old logging road; follow it to the right.
13.5 Singletrack splits downhill at apex of turn. Tired of big bumps? Stay on the logging road. Of a singletrack mind? Bear right.
14.8 Trail and logging road rejoin by the banks of the North Fork of Brackett Creek. Head downhill on road.
15.4 Parking lot on Central Camp Road.

Ross Pass

Location: 17 miles north of Bozeman on the east flank of the Bridger Range. ***See map on page 56.***

Distance: 4.6 miles, one way.

Time: 1.5 to 2.5 hours.

Tread: 3.7 miles on good dirt road; 0.9 mile on doubletrack. Loop option features mostly doubletrack with some singletrack sections.

Aerobic level: Moderate, with a few strenuous pitches.

Technical difficulty: 2 on roads, 3 and 4 on double- and singletrack.

Hazards: Watch for traffic on open roads; storms may come over the Bridger divide without warning.

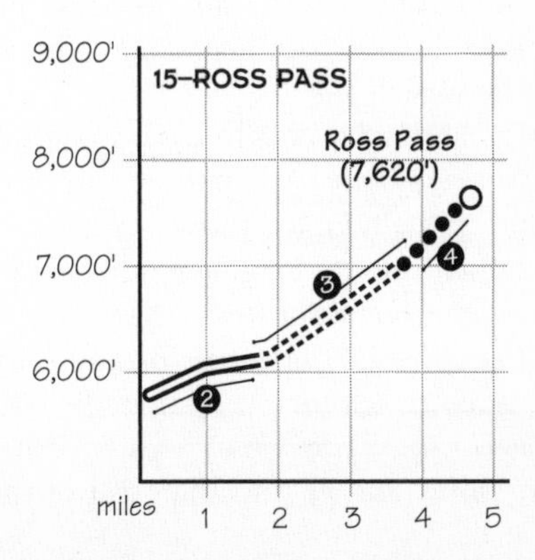

Highlights: The easiest ride to the crest of the Bridger Range; great views from Ross Pass; some fun doubletrack.

Land status: Gallatin National Forest; private.

Maps: Gallatin National Forest; USGS Saddle Peak.

Access: From the corner of Griffin Drive and North Rouse (MT 86) in Bozeman drive 18 miles north on MT 86 to the end of the pavement at the three-way junction at Brackett Creek. Bear right onto Brackett Creek Road and go east 100 yards to a large parking area on the right, just after crossing the creek.

The ride:

0.0 From the parking lot, pedal west to the three-way junction. Go 50 yards north on MT 86 and turn left onto Middle Fork of Brackett Creek Road (FR 6607). This open logging road wanders west then north.

1.1 Central Camp Road goes right; stay left on Middle Fork Road. From here the road rolls southwest, shaded at times by forest.

1.8 Seasonal closure gate (road is open to bikes all year).

2.3 Begin moderate climb and series of looping switchbacks. Look up for occasional glimpses of Ross Peak to the west.

3.1 Just when the road seems to have straightened out it begins twisting madly back on itself and climbing more seriously, especially in the turns.

3.7 Trail 525 (here, an old logging road) exits left and uphill; bear right to aim for Ross Pass.

4.2 One last set of four big ess turns and then the road turns to doubletrack for the final grade to the pass.

4.6 Ross Pass. Enjoy the views west overlooking the Gallatin Valley and east to the crest of the Crazies.

9,004-foot Ross Peak is immediately to the north and summits to the south guard the runs at Bridger Bowl ski area. The Bridger Mountains Foothills Trail (534) runs north and south from the pass, clinging to the west flank of the range. This route is too rocky and steep for all but hikers and mountain goats on full suspension frames. Most folks coast back down the Middle Fork Road, retracing their tracks to the parking lot.

Variation: More adventurous riders can make a loop by dropping east back down the pass and cutting right onto Trail 525 (at mile 3.7 above). This option adds about 0.3 mile to the round-trip distance, not counting getting lost on one of the many spur roads and unofficial trails that beckon around every bend. Some sections may be boggy, even during a mid-summer dry spell.

The logging road dips into a damp gully and contours through an old clearcut. It soon turns to doubletrack and climbs moderately to a spur ridge and a junction with the Pine Slushman Trail to Bridger Bowl. Lean left here and continue on an east-bound beeline downhill. This track eventually drops onto the South Fork Road (FR 631), which is open to motorized traffic from June into October. Turn left; pass a gate and lean into a big, looping right turn in the next 0.3 mile. Follow the road downhill from here to MT 86 and the Brackett Creek parking lot.

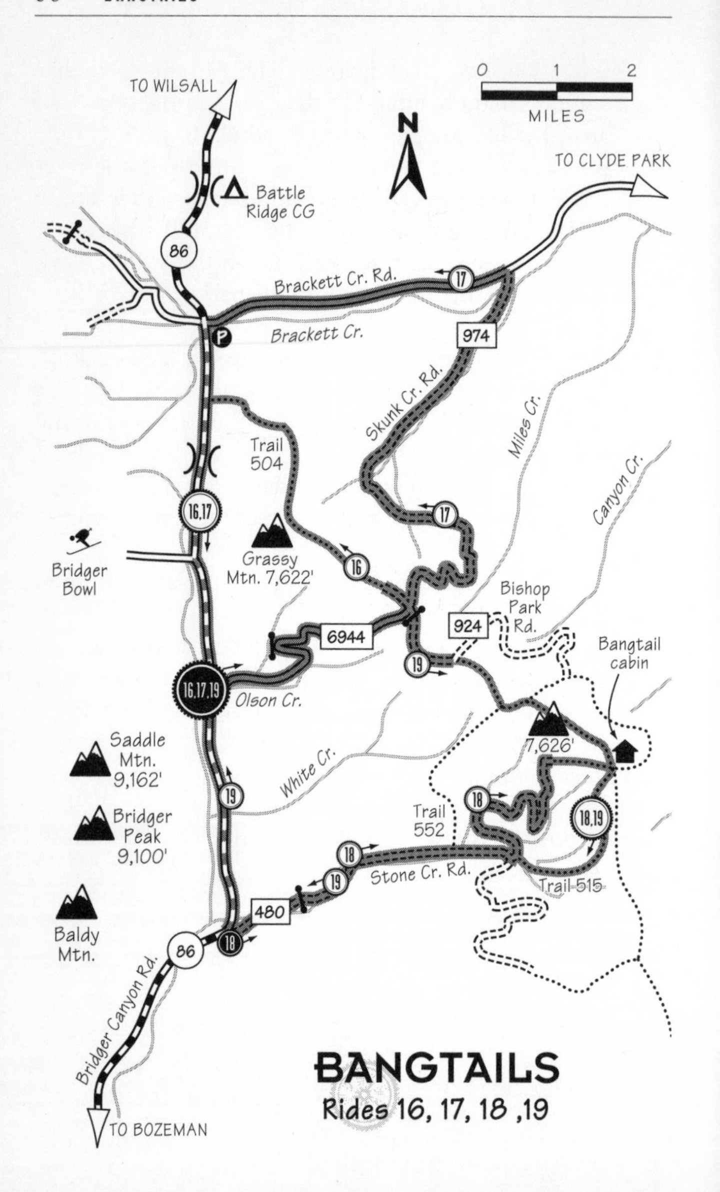

0 1 2
MILES
N
TO WILSALL
TO CLYDE PARK
Battle Ridge CG
86
Brackett Cr. Rd.
17
Brackett Cr.
974
Skunk Cr. Rd.
Miles Cr.
Canyon Cr.
Trail 504
16,17
17
Bridger Bowl
Grassy Mtn. 7,622'
16
Bishop Park Rd.
924
6944
19
Bangtail cabin
16,17,19
Olson Cr.
7,626'
Saddle Mtn. 9,162'
White Cr.
Bridger Peak 9,100'
19
Trail 552
18
18,19
18
19
Stone Cr. Rd.
Trail 515
480
Baldy Mtn.
86
18
Bridger Canyon Rd.
TO BOZEMAN
BANGTAILS
Rides 16, 17, 18 ,19

Grassy Mountain Loop

Location: 12 miles northeast of Bozeman along the crest of the Bangtails in Bridger Canyon.

Distance: 13.3-mile loop.

Time: 1.5 to 2.5 hours.

Tread: 4.1 miles on open logging road; 1.3 miles on doubletrack; 4 miles on singletrack; 3.9 miles on paved road.

Aerobic level: Mostly moderate but with several strenuous climbs.

Technical difficulty: 1 on paved road; 2 and 3 on logging roads and doubletrack; 4 to 4+ on singletrack.

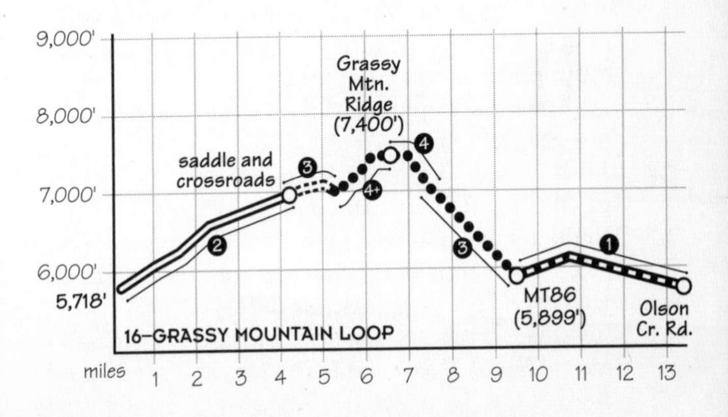

Hazards: Watch for traffic on Olson Creek Road and MT 86. Frequent dips and kelly humps on doubletrack. Smooth, fast singletrack has intervals of rough, rocky sections.

Highlights: Fine singletrack in the unspoiled end of the Bangtails; spectacular views east to the Crazy Mountains and west to the Bridgers.

Land status: Private; Big Sky Lumber; Gallatin National Forest.

Maps: Gallatin National Forest; USGS Grassy Mountain.

Access: From the corner of Griffin Drive and North Rouse in Bozeman drive 13.4 miles north on North Rouse, which becomes Bridger Canyon Road (MT 86) as it leaves town. Watch for Olson Creek Road (FR 6944) on the right (about 2.7 miles north of Stone Creek Road). Park in the gravel pullout on the left (west) side of MT 86.

The ride:

0.0 Cross to the east side of MT 86 and pedal up gravel Olson Creek Road (FR 6944). The road climbs moderately, twisting in and out of gullies on the south-facing hillside. CAUTION: Watch for logging trucks and other traffic, especially on blind turns.

1.6 Jeep track goes uphill and right at apex of a hairpin turn. Stay left on main road.

2.2 North Fork of Olson Creek Road (FR 9651) goes left (gated); stay right on main road.

2.7 Doubletrack scrambles uphill on left; stay on main road. Olson Creek Road bends northeast through an old clearcut and the grade eases slightly.

4.1 Crossroads in an open saddle. (Straight—northeast—leads to Skunk Creek and Ride 17; right—southeast—

and past the gate connects with roads and trails in the Stone Creek drainage; see rides 18 and 19.) Turn left on the jeep doubletrack and pedal northwest through a grassy park. The track climbs in spurts to a low ridge. Several dips and kelly humps cut across the roadbed.

4.3 Spur goes right; stay left on main track.

4.5 Spur goes right; stay left.

4.8 Spur goes right; stay left, bearing west.

5.0 Top of low ridge. Here the doubletrack swoops down through a recently logged-over stand of pine and fir—watch for debris and rough tread.

5.3 The trail enters a small meadow and bends north.

5.4 0.1-mile strenuous climb on steep, loose, twinned singletrack.

5.5 Another meadow; the grade eases.

5.6 Climb onto logging road, leaning right (north).

5.7 Turn left and uphill on singletrack. Don't be fooled here by knobby tracks continuing right on the road—it deadends in about 0.3 mile. Shift down for the strenuous singletrack climb onto Grassy Mountain's main ridge. The tread grows rocky and loose (4+) near the top.

6.1 Grade eases and contours north along the east flank of Grassy Mountain at about 7,400 feet, with good views east to the Crazies and the Shields Valley. Tread from here on out tends to be narrow with occasional rocky sections.

6.4 Steep (!) but short climb to saddle on the ridge.

6.5 Drop into westside meadows with outstanding views of Ross Peak and Pass in the Bridgers.

6.7 Cross through another shallow saddle to east side.

7.0 Drop sharply (it's rocky, a -4) onto west slope and begin long descent.

7.3 Trail banks into trees and easy, open switchbacks.

7.9 Abrupt whoop-de-doo around tree. Then a spur trail goes right and uphill to a great view west of the Bridgers. Continue left, down the main trail through open forest.

8.4 CAUTION: Trail banks left and straight down the fall line. Stop and dismount before you make the turn. Please use restraint and walk down this short but steep (!) drop; it can't be ridden without skidding and too many knobbies have scraped off any plants that grew here. From here the tread is mostly smooth and sinuous through deep forest—a slice of fat tire heaven.

9.4 The trail breaks out of the trees and curves left to drop down to MT 86. CAUTION: The trail is rutted and joins the pavement at an angle—it's difficult to watch for cars on the road as you drop onto it. Turn left and pedal south on MT 86, climbing moderately at first.

10.6 Top of grade; begin fast descent into upper Bridger Canyon.

11.9 Bridger Bowl access road on right; stay on MT 86.

13.3 Olson Creek Road and parking pullout on right.

Skunk Creek Loop

Location: 14 miles north of Bozeman, over the Bangtail Divide and back up Brackett Creek. ***See map on page 66.***

Distance: 18.6-mile loop.

Time: 2.5 to 4 hours.

Tread: 10.3 miles on open logging road and jeep track; 3.8 miles on gravel highway; and 4.5 miles on pavement.

Aerobic level: Moderate.

Technical difficulty: 1 on paved roads; 2 on gravel roads.

Hazards: Watch for traffic and logging trucks; Skunk Creek Road may be rough in places, especially on upper sections.

Highlights: A long but non-technical road ride with great views of the Crazy Mountains.

Land status: Gallatin National Forest; Big Sky Lumber; private.

Maps: Gallatin National Forest; USGS Grassy Mountain, Saddle Peak.

Access: From the corner of Griffin Drive and North Rouse in Bozeman drive 13.4 miles north on North Rouse, which becomes Bridger Canyon Road (MT 86) as it leaves town. Watch for Olson Creek Road (FR 6944) on the right (about 2.7 miles north of Stone Creek Road). Park in the gravel pullout on the left (west) side of MT 86.

The ride:

0.0 Cross to the east side of MT 86 and pedal up gravel Olson Creek Road (FR 6944). The road climbs moderately, twisting in and out of gullies on the south-facing hillside. CAUTION: Watch for logging trucks and other traffic, especially on blind turns.

1.6 Jeep track goes uphill and right at apex of a hairpin turn. Stay left on main road.

2.2 North Fork of Olson Creek Road (FR 9651) goes left (gated); stay right on main road.

2.7 Doubletrack scrambles uphill on left; stay on main road. Olson Creek Road bends northeast through an old clearcut and the grade eases slightly.

4.1 Crossroads in an open saddle. Veer slightly left as the main road climbs northeast (the gated Bishop Park Road goes hard right).

4.3 Spur goes left; stay right (enjoy the view from 7,123 feet), and begin a fast drop into the head of Miles Creek. The road drops hard in a handful of tight turns over the next 1.5 miles.

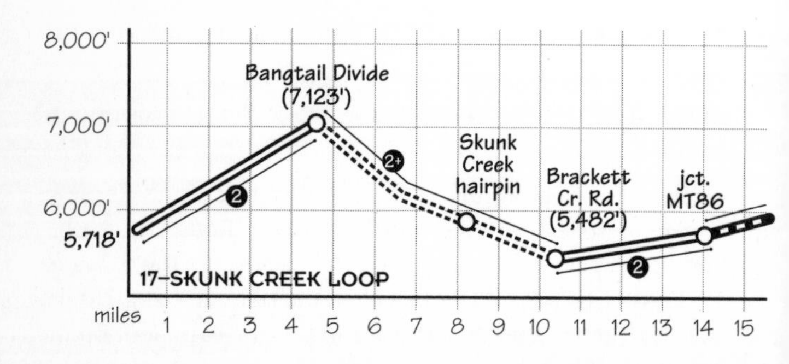

6.3 Grade eases and then rolls north, with one notable but brief climb, before dropping into the Skunk Creek drainage.
8.1 A big hairpin turn loops across Skunk Creek and the road beelines along the north bank of the creek.
9.9 Spur goes right; stay straight on main road.
10.3 Turn left onto gravel Brackett Creek Road and pedal west; CAUTION: Watch for traffic.
14.1 Three-way junction. Turn left onto paved MT 86 and begin steady climb south.
16.6 Top of pass; enjoy the downhill run.
18.6 Olson Creek Road and parking pullout.

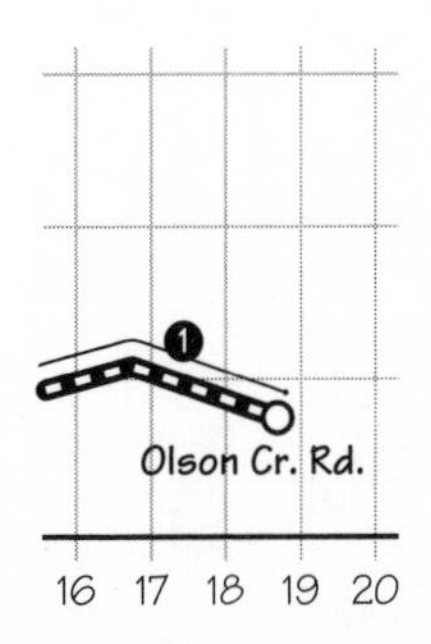

Stone Creek Loop

Location: 11 miles north of Bozeman in Bridger Canyon, in the Bangtail Range. ***See map on page 66.***

Distance: 13.6 miles.

Time: 1.5 to 2.5 hours.

Tread: 11.1 miles on jeep road; 2.5 miles on singletrack.

Aerobic level: Moderate to strenuous.

Technical difficulty: 2 on gravel road; 3 to 4 on singletrack.

Hazards: Enjoy the descent but ride in control—some sections are steep and loose with abrupt turns.

Highlights: Challenging singletrack climbs and descents; great views from the Bangtail Cabin.

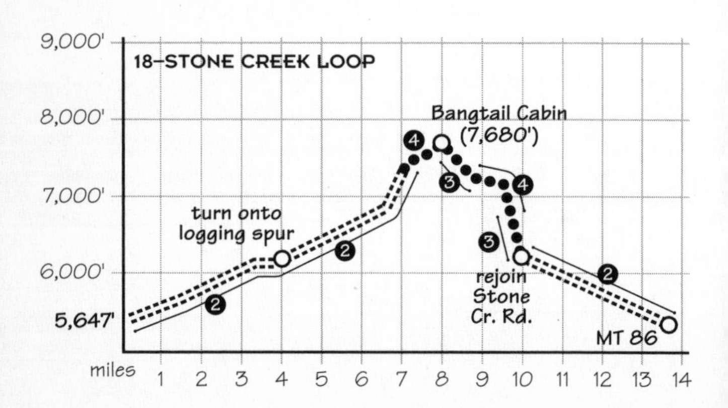

Land status: Gallatin National Forest; Big Sky Lumber; private.

Maps: Gallatin National Forest; USGS Grassy Mountain.

Access: From the corner of Griffin Drive and North Rouse in Bozeman drive 10.7 miles north on North Rouse, which becomes Bridger Canyon Road (MT 86) as it leaves town. Watch for Stone Creek Road (FR 480) on the right. Park on the gravel shoulders of the Stone Creek Road where it meets MT 86.

The ride:

0.0 Pedal east up Stone Creek Road as it climbs easily on the north bank of the creek. The road gains only 700 feet in elevation over its first 3.7 miles.

1.4 Forest Service gate across road.

3.3 Moody Creek Trail goes left and uphill—this is an optional return leg for the loop. For now, stay on the easy grade of the main road.

3.6 Just before the main road makes a big hairpin around the two forks of Stone Creek, bank left onto a logging spur road. Some locals call this road "Nick's Nightmare," and it can induce that lost-in-a-maze dread common to some folks' dreams. The road snakes north, west, north, and south before ever turning east toward its goal, and then it wraps around itself again. But the grade is moderate compared to neighboring trails, and the views on top are worth it.

5.7 Spur goes left; steer right.

6.6 Spur goes right; steer left and begin steady climb north.

7.0 Road turns east and contours on an easier grade.

7.3 Road ends. Continue east on singletrack, which soon climbs one last pitch to the Bangtail Divide.

8.0 The trail tops out on old jeep track just south of the Bangtail Cabin (7,680 feet). The cabin makes a good rest stop and boasts great views east to the Crazies. From here there are two possible return routes: north 1.9 miles along the Bangtail Divide trail (single- and doubletrack) and then west and down the steep, technical (4+) Moody Creek trail, or south on jeep track to Stone Creek Trail 515. Gonzo downhillers will like Moody Creek; the rest of us can drop south toward Stone Creek.

8.1 Turn right onto Trail 515 where the Bishop Park Road comes in from the left. Trail 515 drops in a fast line across the slope, then rolls south and across the head of Stone Creek (a sometimes boggy spot).

8.8 The trail drops again through a series of broad but plunging switchbacks, contours briefly, and then zig zags down to the creek.

9.5 Stream crossing; grade eases.

9.8 Stream crossing.

9.9 Rejoin Stone Creek Road. Bank onto the road and head downhill.

13.6 Junction with MT 86.

Olson-Stone Loop

Location: 14 miles north of Bozeman along the Bangtail Divide. ***See map on page 66.***

Distance: 15.5-mile loop.

Time: 2 to 3 hours.

Tread: 2.7 miles on paved road; 7.8 on gravel roads; 5 miles on double- and singletrack.

Aerobic level: Moderate.

Technical difficulty: 1 on paved road; 2 on gravel roads; 3 to 4+ on single- and doubletrack.

Hazards: Watch for traffic on open roads; logging activity may alter or wipe out established trails.

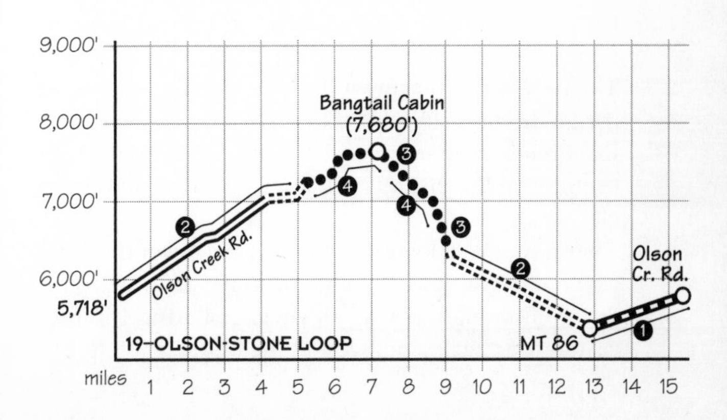

Highlights: Several sections of good singletrack; outstanding views from along the Bangtail crest and around the Bangtail Cabin.

Land status: Gallatin National Forest; Big Sky Lumber; private.

Maps: Gallatin National Forest; USGS Grassy Mountain.

Access: From the corner of Griffin Drive and North Rouse in Bozeman drive 13.4 miles north on North Rouse, which becomes Bridger Canyon Road (MT 86) as it leaves town. Watch for Olson Creek Road (FR 6944) on the right (about 2.7 miles north of Stone Creek Road). Park in the gravel pullout on the left (west) side of MT 86.

The ride:

0.0 Cross to the east side of MT 86 and pedal up gravel Olson Creek Road (FR 6944). The road climbs moderately, twisting in and out of gullies on the south-facing hillside. CAUTION: Watch for logging trucks and other traffic, especially on blind turns.

2.2 North Fork of Olson Creek Road (FR 9651) goes left (gated); stay right on main road.

2.7 The road bends northeast through an old clearcut and the grade eases slightly.

4.1 Crossroads in an open saddle. Pedal up and right, past the gate on the Bishop Park Road (FR 974) and into a clearcut.

4.9 After rounding a low rise and dropping down the other side, cut right onto a doubletrack into the trees. This trail rolls along the Bangtail Divide, offering glimpses east to the Crazies and west to the Bridgers.

5.7 Moody Creek Trail drops off to the right (an old-fashioned roller coaster ride down to the Stone Creek Road). Stay straight on the divide trail.
6.1 Hook right and climb hard for 0.2 mile; the grade eases near the top.
6.4 Spur road goes left; stay right on singletrack and pedal downhill and south as the trail favors the west side of the ridge.
7.1 The Bangtail Cabin (7,680 feet)—a good spot for lunch and taking in the vistas. From here pedal south, past the first singletrack breaking right.
7.2 Turn right onto Trail 515 where the Bishop Park Road comes in from the left. Trail 515 drops in a fast line across the slope, then rolls south and across the head of Stone Creek (a sometimes boggy spot).
8.0 The trail drops again through a series of broad but plunging switchbacks, contours briefly, and then zig zags down to the creek.
8.7 Stream crossing; grade eases.
9.0 Stream crossing.
9.1 Bank onto Stone Creek Road and head downhill.
12.8 Turn right on Bridger Canyon Road (MT 86) and pedal north.
15.5 Olson Creek Road.

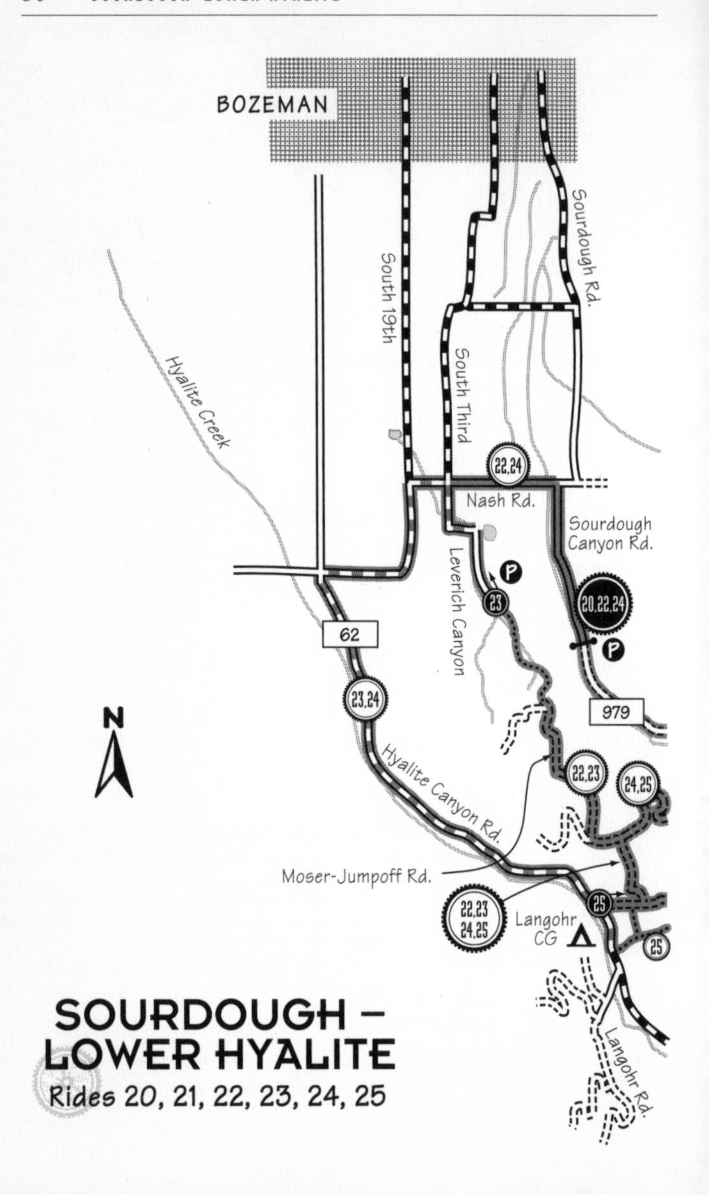

SOURDOUGH – LOWER HYALITE

Rides 20, 21, 22, 23, 24, 25

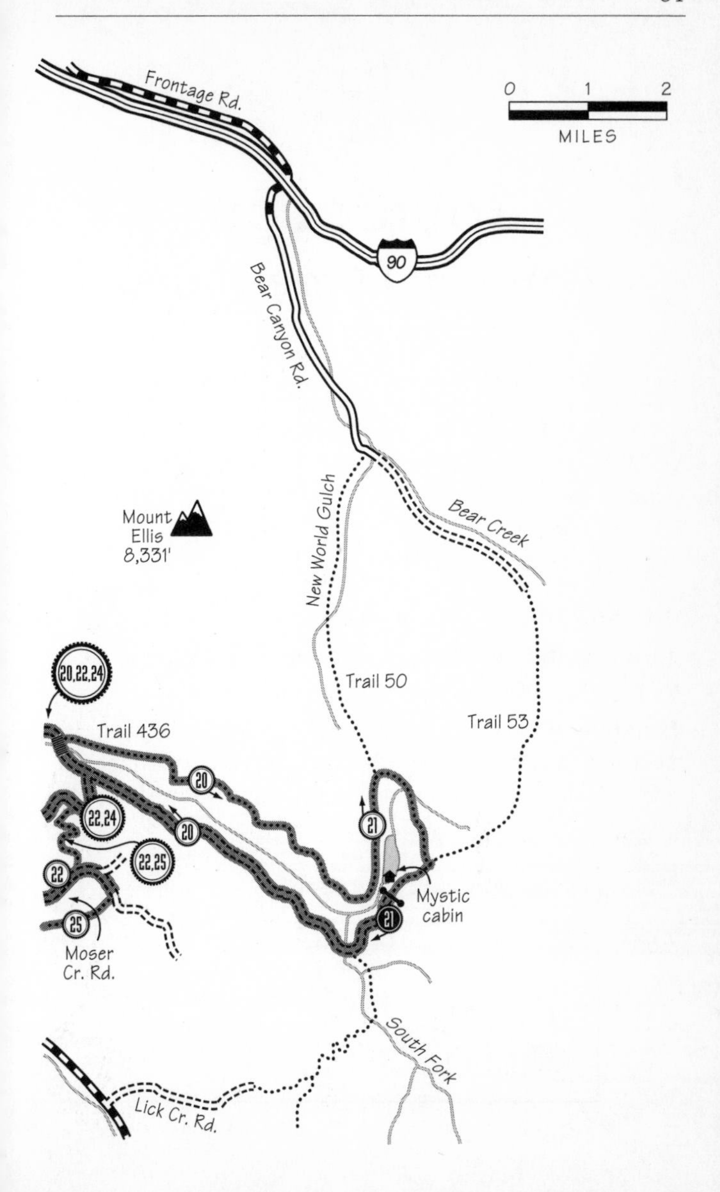
Frontage Rd.
0 1 2
MILES
90
Bear Canyon Rd.
New World Gulch
Bear Creek
Mount Ellis
8,331'
Trail 50
Trail 53
20,22,24
Trail 436
20
22,24
20
21
22,25
22
Mystic cabin
21
25
Moser Cr. Rd.
South Fork
Lick Cr. Rd.

Sourdough (Bozeman) Creek Loop

Location: 7 miles south of Bozeman in the foothills of the Gallatin Range. ***See map on page 80.***

Distance: 17.6 miles round trip.

Time: 2 to 3 hours.

Tread: 14.7 miles on smooth, gated doubletrack; 2.9 miles on superb singletrack.

Aerobic level: Moderate to strenuous.

Technical difficulty: 2 on roads; 3 to 4 on singletrack, with long sections of steep, exposed sidehill.

Hazards: Watch for other trail users; this route receives heavy bike, foot, and horse traffic, especially on road near trailhead. Schedule your visit during mid-week or other low-use times.

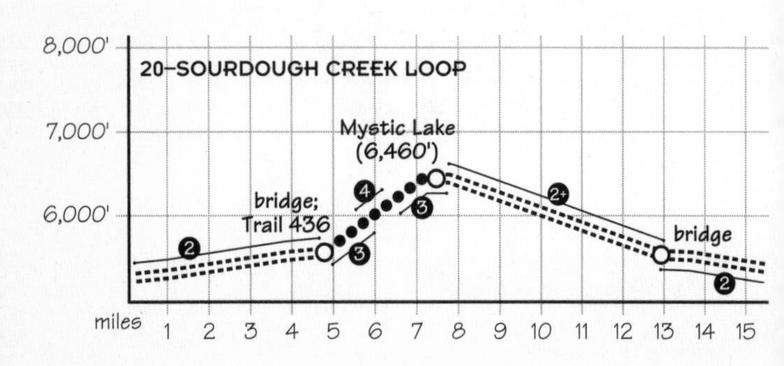

Narrow trail crosses long, exposed sidehill on singletrack option.

Highlights: Gradual climb into scenic, shady forest; Mystic Lake; challenging but fun singletrack; and a long, fast descent on a gravel road.

Land status: Gallatin National Forest; City of Bozeman.

Maps: Gallatin National Forest; USGS Bozeman, Wheeler Mountain, Mount Ellis. (Sourdough Creek is shown as Bozeman Creek on more recent maps and signs.)

Access: From East Main Street in Bozeman drive 1.6 miles south on South Church, which becomes Sourdough Road as it leaves town. Go straight at the intersection with Kagy Boulevard and continue 5.4 miles south on Sourdough Road (pavement ends in 4.8 miles). Turn right onto Nash Road, drive 0.2 mile west, and turn left onto Sourdough Canyon Road (the sign may be hard to see). Watch for car-eating potholes and other traffic. Drive 1 mile south to the parking lot and trailhead at road's end.

The ride:

0.0 Parking lot and gate across old roadway (FR 979). Pedal around the gate and south along Sourdough (Bozeman) Creek. As it climbs away from the trailhead, this old road is reverting to doubletrack. But if a pending timber sale goes through, the road will be re-graded. For now, stay on the right-hand side and watch for oncoming trail users.

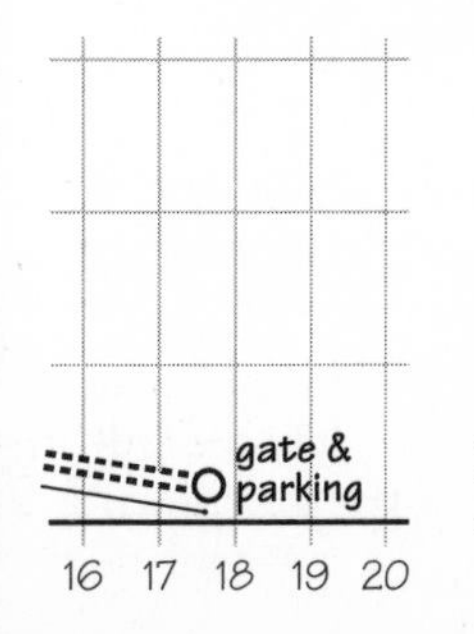

2.7 Outhouse on right.

4.4 Begin descent through broad

curves; watch for muddy spot at bottom.

4.7 The Bridge. Trail 436 goes left, marked by a sign advising mountain bikers to watch for other trail users and yield the right-of-way. Riders who want to avoid singletrack should stay on the main road, which reaches Mystic Lake in about 5.2 miles (the road leg is also our return route; see miles 7.7 to 12.9 below). Instead, let's tackle the singletrack climb. Lean left and pedal into the trees on Trail 436. The grade is fairly easy at first.

5.2 0.2-mile stretch of exposed sidehill on steep slope.

5.5 Short moderately strenuous climb.

6.0 0.2-mile stretch of exposed sidehill on steep slope.

6.2 Rock outcrop; trail bends left into lush ravine, then climbs through trees; some roots in trail.

6.5 Trail meanders east-southeast, bearing toward Mystic Lake.

6.7 The next 0.6 mile of trail is fairly smooth but has intervals of off-camber tread on exposed sidehill.

7.1 Big looping switchback right.

7.5 First glimpse of Mystic Lake.

7.6 Spillway road at west end of lake (6,460 feet). Left leads around the lake (see Ride 21) and to New World Gulch and Bear Canyon. Turn right and cross the spillway. The doubletrack bends toward the cabin on the southwest shore; watch for a track breaking right that meets the main road (FR 979).

7.7 Turn right on FR 979 and begin a long coast downhill. The road bends south high above the creek before dropping to a big hairpin turn where it meets...

9.2 The South Fork of Sourdough Creek and Hood Creek Trail 436 (in the form of a spur road on the left; see Ride 23). Bear right on FR 979 and continue the wild downhill run.

12.7 Spur road goes left; sign for Hyalite Divide. (Access to Moser Creek trails, and Hyalite and Leverich canyons—see rides 22, 23, 24, and 25.) Lean right.

12.9 The Bridge again. Bank left on the main road and pedal up the last real climb before dropping out the final 4 miles.

17.6 Gate and parking lot.

Mystic Lake Loop

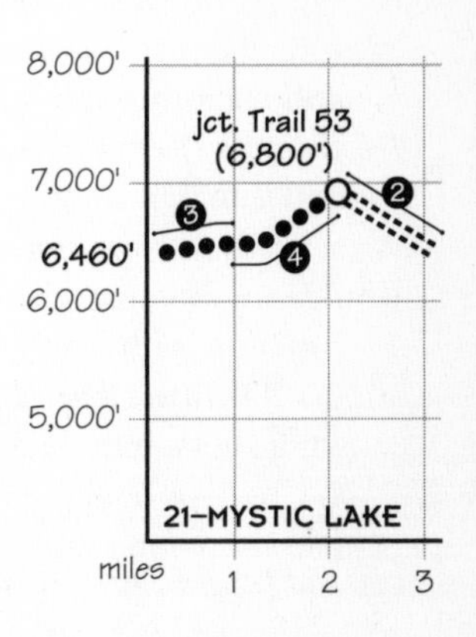

Location: 10 miles southeast of Bozeman around the shores of Mystic Lake. ***See map on page 80.***

Distance: 3-mile loop.

Time: 1 to 1.5 hours.

Tread: 2 miles on rough singletrack; 1 mile on logging road doubletrack.

Aerobic level: Moderate to strenuous.

Technical difficulty: 2 on logging road; 3 to 4 on singletrack, with a spot or two of 5.

Hazards: Some obstacles on trail come up suddenly; see mile-by-mile description.

Land status: Gallatin National Forest; City of Bozeman.

Maps: Gallatin National Forest; USGS Mount Ellis.

Access: This loop is an extension of the Sourdough Creek tour (Ride 20). Pedaling in to Mystic Lake is the only way to access this route, and Sourdough Creek offers the only practical approach.

The ride:

0.0 Pedal east across the spillway to the junction with Trail 436 on the left. Lean right and follow the sandy doubletrack up and into the trees. The route turns into singletrack as it winds through the trees north of the lake.

0.8 Big (!) drop off a root step. Then a sharp, square-bottomed cut across the trail—probably best to dismount and walk through both of these obstacles. And maybe through the grassy bog, too, where the trail winds right and then left again into the trees.

0.9 Short but strenuous climb.

1.0 Stream crossing; then climb hard.

1.1 Junction with New World Gulch Trail 50 (see Appendix A). Turn right onto Mystic Cabin Trail and hold on for a short, bumpy downhill.

1.2 0.1 mile of boggy sections; two stream crossings. The lakeshore ran close to the trail here before the spillway was breached. After the second stream crossing, portage your bike up the steep bank of the gully—it's often chopped by packstock into rough, unrideable steps. From here the trail rolls through forest, with occasional moderate climbs.

1.8 Stream crossing.

2.0 Signed junction with Bear Lakes Trail 53, an old logging road (at 6,800 feet). Turn right and follow this grassy doubletrack downhill toward the southwest end of Mystic Lake.

2.6 Bar gate across the road.

2.9 Blue blaze marks the singletrack that splits right and back toward Mystic Cabin. Turn right here and then cross the spillway to complete the loop. Or stay on the main road (which becomes FR 979) for an enjoyable 10-mile downhill run to the Sourdough Creek trailhead (see Ride 20).

Leverich Loop A:
Sourdough Creek Road

Location: 7 miles south of Bozeman in the foothills of the Gallatin Range. ***See map on page 80.***

Distance: 17.4-mile loop.

Time: 1.5 to 3 hours (add at least an hour if you ride from town).

Tread: 1 mile on pavement; 7.8 miles on gravel roads open to traffic; 6.1 miles on closed doubletrack; 3.5 miles on singletrack.

Aerobic level: Easy to moderate; 0.3-mile strenuous climb if you take the singletrack option.

Technical difficulty: 1 and 2 on logging roads; 3 and 4 in Leverich Canyon.

Hazards: Watch for traffic on Nash Road; steep, fall-away switchbacks on upper singletrack; heavy trail use in lower Sourdough and Leverich canyons.

Highlights: Good views of Bozeman and Gallatin Valley; fun singletrack with ample adrenaline rush opportunities.

Land status: Gallatin National Forest, City of Bozeman; private.

Maps: Gallatin National Forest; USGS Wheeler Mountain, Mount Ellis.

Access: From East Main Street in Bozeman drive 1.6 miles south on South Church, which becomes Sourdough Road as it leaves town. Go straight at the intersection with Kagy Boulevard and continue 3.8 miles south on Sourdough Road (pavement ends in 3.2 miles). Turn right on Nash, drive 0.2 mile west, and turn left (south) on Sourdough Canyon Road (it's marked but the sign may be hard to see). Watch for car-eating potholes and other traffic. Drive 1 mile south to the parking lot and trailhead at road's end.

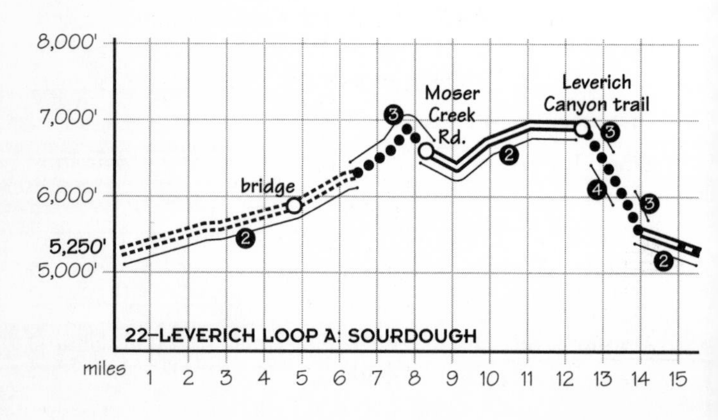

Sprocket rocketeers can bike it from town, riding out and back on South Third to avoid traffic. This adds about 13 miles total to the ride. From Kagy Boulevard, pedal 0.8 mile south on South Third. The road ahead becomes Wagon Wheel. Turn right to stay on South Third, which then bends south again. Continue 1.3 miles south and turn right on Goldenstein Road. Go 0.1 mile west and turn left onto South Third. Go 2.1 miles south, turn left onto Nash Road, and ride 1.5 miles to Sourdough Canyon Road. Turn right and pedal 1 mile south to the trailhead at road's end.

The ride:

0.0 Trailhead and gate on Sourdough Creek Road (FR 979). Pedal south on doubletrack as it climbs gently along Sourdough (Bozeman) Creek. CAUTION: Watch for other trail users. Ride in control and yield to all hikers and equestrians.

2.7 Outhouse on right. Continue straight on main road.

4.4 Enjoy a breezy, curvy descent. Watch for muddy spot at bottom.

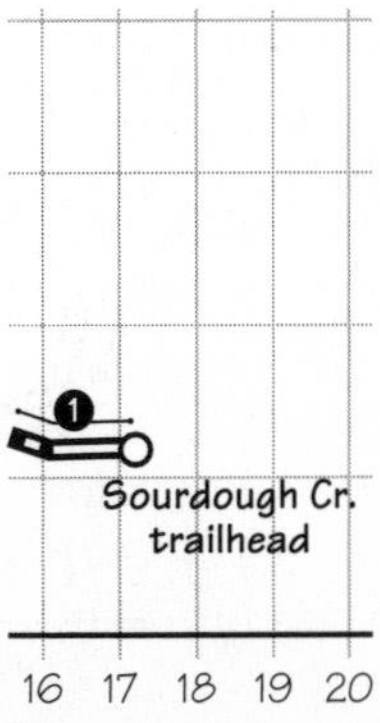

4.7 Right turn, sign for mountain bikers, and bridge. Trail 436 leaves road on east side of creek. Stay on main road and cross bridge.

4.9 Turn right on old logging road (first right after bridge). Sign points to Hyalite Divide.

5.4 Climb through two big hairpin turns, left then right.

6.1 Flip a coin. Heads, we go left onto singletrack, following the Hyalite Challenge race course. Tails stays

1
Sourdough Cr.
trailhead
16 17 18 19 20

right, climbing 3 miles on the logging road through old clearcuts to a gate and junction with the Moser Jumpoff Road. (Both of these routes are described in Ride 25). Heads it is; the scenic route to the Moser Jumpoff Road. Bear left and begin a moderate climb through broad switchbacks on singletrack that follows an old, overgrown road bed.

6.6 Grade eases slightly.

6.9 Small stream crossing; may be boggy.

7.4 Turn right and uphill off road bed onto singletrack. Trail climbs steeply 0.3 mile to ridgetop clearcut.

7.7 Top of climb (6,820 feet); bear left.

7.8 Spur goes right; stay to left and descend rutted, bumpy hillside.

8.1 Junction with Moser Creek Road. Go right (downhill).

9.0 Turn right on Moser Jumpoff Road. Pedal uphill 0.8 mile to...

9.8 Gated road to Bozeman (Sourdough) Creek on right (if you took tails at mile 6.1, this is where you rejoin our narrative). Go left on the Moser Jumpoff Road and continue steady climb.

10.0 Grade eases; good views south to Mount Blackmore and The Mummy.

10.3 Spur roads on left; stay right, following signs for FR 3159. Resume climb.

10.7 Enjoy brief descent and then level grade.

10.9 Spur road on right; stay left.

11.2 Spur road on right; stay left.

11.4 Spur road on right; stay left. The grade gives way to an easy 0.5-mile downhill.

12.4 First glimpse of Bozeman (from 6,880 feet); watch for sign marking Leverich Canyon Trail 426 on right. Drop onto singletrack and flex over six sharp (but fun) kelly humps.

12.5 Bank right and hang on. The next 0.6 mile features steep drops, down-the-fall-line switchbacks, and somewhat rocky tread. It's all rideable, but sling your butt over the rear tire to avoid skidding (to save the trail) and keep those brake pads on the rims (to save your butt).

13.0 Pass an old mine and cabin, then swing through one last vertigo-inducing switchback to the left.

13.1 Bounce down to a right-hand hairpin turn through a shallow stream. From here the descent is more moderate, following the gradient of Leverich Creek. Foot and horse traffic also are heavier on this stretch.

13.4 Two shallow stream crossings.

13.7 Water bars and boggy spots.

13.8 Stream crossings, often muddy.

13.9 One last stream crossing and you're in the trailhead parking lot. Pedal north on the one-lane, heavily graveled road.

14.9 Ride past big red barn onto pavement. The road skirts a pond, swings west, then runs north again.

15.9 Junction with Nash Road and South Third. Go straight north to ride back to town. If your car is parked at the Sourdough Creek trailhead, turn right onto gravel Nash Road.

16.4 Turn right (south) onto Sourdough Canyon Road.

17.4 Parking lot and trailhead.

Leverich Loop B:
Hyalite Canyon Road

Location: 9 miles south of Bozeman in the foothills of the Gallatin Range. ***See map on page 80.***

Distance: 15.9-mile loop.

Time: 1.5 to 3 hours.

Tread: 9.4 miles on paved roads; 5 miles on gravel roads open to traffic; 1.5 miles on singletrack.

Aerobic level: Easy to moderate.

Technical difficulty: 1 on paved and gravel roads; 3 to 4 in Leverich Canyon.

Hazards: Watch for traffic on roads; steep, fall-away

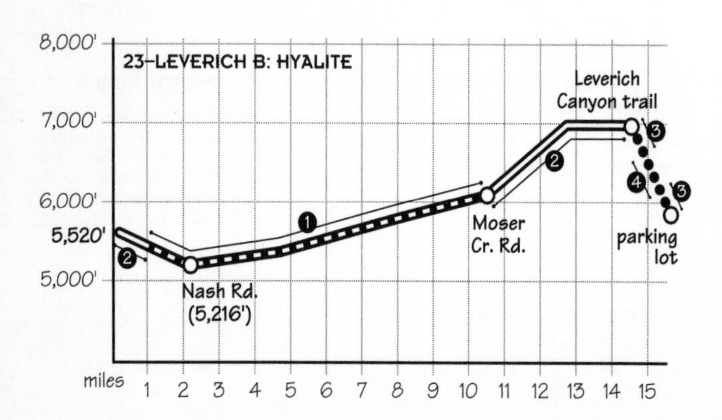

switchbacks on upper singletrack; heavy trail use in lower Leverich Canyon.

Highlights: Good views of Bozeman and Gallatin Valley; fun singletrack with ample adrenaline rush opportunities. This route offers an easier approach to the Leverich Canyon Singletrack (see Ride 22).

Land status: Gallatin National Forest; private.

Maps: Gallatin National Forest; USGS Wheeler Mountain.

Access: From Kagy Boulevard in Bozeman drive 0.8 mile south on South Third. The road ahead becomes Wagon Wheel. Turn right to stay on South Third, which then bends south again. Continue 1.3 miles south and turn right on Goldenstein Road. Go 0.1 mile west and turn left onto South Third. Go 2.1 miles south to the intersection with Nash Road. Go straight (south); the road becomes Leverich Canyon Road and winds east then south again. The pavement ends at a big red barn about 1 mile from Nash. Continue 1 mile south on the heavily graveled one-lane road to the parking lot and trailhead at road's end.

The ride:

0.0 Pedal north on the gravel and paved road back to Nash Road.

2.0 Turn left (west) on Nash.

2.5 Turn left (south) on South 19th. CAUTION: Watch for high-speed traffic. Follow the road around the big turn west at Kirk Hill and continue to...

4.6 Paved Hyalite Canyon Road (FR 62). Turn left and pedal into Hyalite Canyon on this smooth, winding highway above the creek. Watch for traffic, especially on blind turns.

10.4 Turn left (east) onto gravel Moser Creek Road (FR 3160).

11.0 Turn left (north) onto Moser Jumpoff Road (FR 3159) and begin moderate climb.
11.8 Gated road to Bozeman Creek on right; bear left to stay on Moser Jumpoff Road.
12.0 Grade eases; good views south to Mount Blackmore and The Mummy.
12.3 Spur roads on left; stay right, following sign for FR 3159. Resume climb.
12.7 Enjoy brief descent and then level grade.
12.9 Spur road on right; stay left.
13.2 Spur road on right; stay left.
13.4 Spur road on right; stay left. The grade gives way to an easy 0.5-mile downhill.
14.4 First glimpse of Bozeman (from 6,880 feet); watch for sign marking Leverich Canyon Trail 426 on right. Drop onto singletrack and flex over six sharp (but fun) kelly humps.
14.5 Bank right and hang on. The next 0.6 mile features steep drops, down-the-fall-line switchbacks, and somewhat rocky tread. It's all rideable, but sling your butt over the rear tire to avoid skidding (to save the trail) and keep those brake pads on the rims (to save your butt).
15.0 Pass an old mine and cabin, then swing through one last vertigo-inducing switchback to the left.
15.1 Bounce down to a right-hand hairpin turn through a shallow stream. From here the descent is more moderate, following the gradient of Leverich Creek. Foot and horse traffic also are heavier on this stretch.
15.4 Two shallow stream crossings.
15.7 Water bars and boggy spots.
15.8 Stream crossings, often muddy.
15.9 One last stream crossing and you're in the trailhead parking lot.

Lower Hyalite–Sourdough Loop

Location: 8 miles south of Bozeman in the foothills of the Gallatin Range. ***See map on page 80.***

Distance: 21.2-mile loop.

Time: 2.5 to 4 hours.

Tread: 8.4 miles on paved road; 3.9 miles on gravel roads open to traffic; 8.9 miles on closed logging road, some of which is reverting to double- and singletrack.

Aerobic level: Easy, with 1.4 miles of moderate climbing.

Technical difficulty: 1 and 2.

Hazards: Watch for traffic on all open roads; yield to other trail users, especially on popular doubletrack in Sourdough Canyon.

Highlights: A non-technical loop ride in the mountains; an exhilarating 4-mile descent on closed logging roads; many options for side trips or extended loops.

Land status: Gallatin National Forest; City of Bozeman; private.

Maps: Gallatin National Forest; USGS Mount Ellis, Wheeler Mountain.

Access: From East Main Street in Bozeman drive 1.6 miles south on South Church, which becomes Sourdough Road as it leaves town. Go straight at the intersection with Kagy Boulevard and continue 3.8 miles south on Sourdough Road (pavement ends in 3.2 miles). Turn right on Nash, drive 0.2 mile west, and turn left (south) on Sourdough Canyon Road (it's marked but the sign may be hard to see). Watch for car-eating potholes and other traffic. Drive 1 mile south to the parking lot and trailhead at road's end.

The ride:

0.0 Do the unexpected and pedal north, back down the access road.
1.0 Turn left on Nash Road and pedal west.
3.0 Turn left onto South 19th and pedal 2.1 miles south and west.
5.1 Turn left on Hyalite Canyon Road (FR 62) and pedal into the canyon. Watch for traffic but don't let it distract from the scenery and smooth pavement.
10.9 Turn left onto gravel Moser Creek Road (FR 3160) and begin moderate climb.
11.5 Turn left onto Moser Jumpoff Road (FR 3159) and continue climbing.

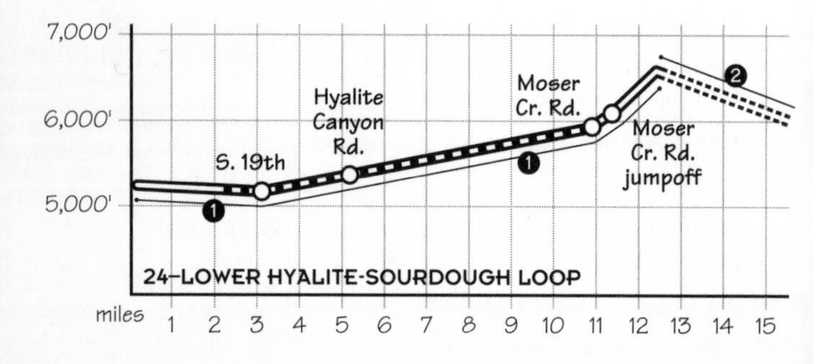

12.3 Turn right at sign for Bozeman (Sourdough) Creek (6,670 feet). Pass through gate and begin long, sweet descent on this old logging road. In places it's reverting to singletrack, but there's plenty of maneuvering room. If a pending timber sale goes through, the road will be re-graded.

13.3 Spur road on left; stay on main route straight ahead.

14.1 Slight uphill for 0.1 mile. Then the road swoops down into a glade of old trees and bottoms out in a hairpin turn to the left. Continue downhill through two more hairpin turns.

16.5 Turn left on Sourdough Creek Road (FR 979), cross the bridge, and pedal north on main doubletrack, climbing for 0.3 mile.

16.8 Resume descent.

18.5 Outhouse on right. Continue straight on main road. CAUTION: Watch for other trail users. Ride in control and yield to all hikers and equestrians.

21.2 Trailhead and parking lot.

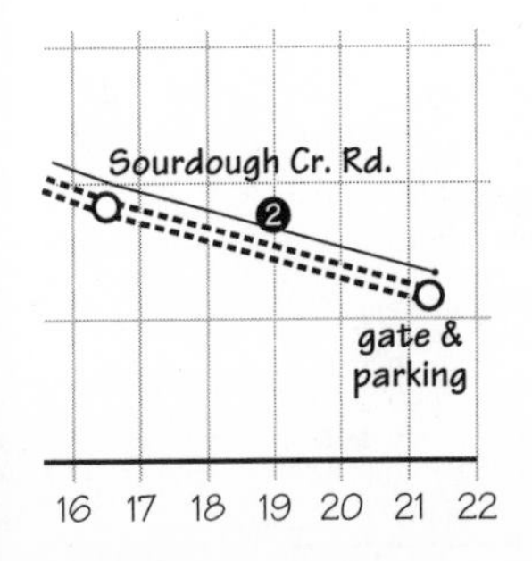

Moser Creek Loop

Location: 10 miles south of Bozeman on the divide between Hyalite and Bozeman creeks. ***See map on page 80.***

Distance: 9.6 miles.

Time: 1 to 2 hours.

Tread: 2.9 miles on open, gravel Forest Road; 3 miles on old logging road; and 3.7 miles on singletrack.

Aerobic level: Moderate, except for a 0.3-mile strenuous climb at the 6-mile mark.

Technical difficulty: Mostly 2 with 1 mile of 3 on the singletrack ascent.

Hazards: Watch for traffic on Hyalite and Moser Creek roads. Go slow on kelly humps

Highlights: Long, fast downhill runs

Land status: Gallatin National Forest; City of Bozeman.

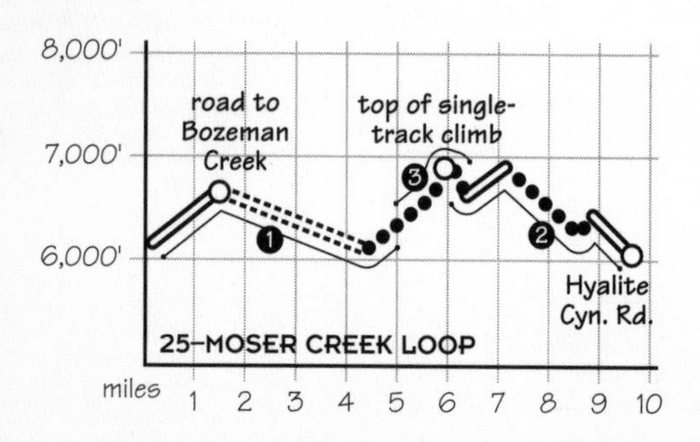

Maps: Gallatin National Forest; USGS Wheeler Mountain, Mount Ellis, Fridley Peak.

Access: From the corner of South 19th and Kagy Boulevard on the southwest edge of Bozeman, drive 6 miles south on South 19th. Turn left (south) on paved Hyalite Canyon Road (FR 62) and drive 5.7 miles to Moser Creek Road (FR 3160) on the left. Park on the shoulder of this narrow gravel road (or drive 0.6 mile uphill to the junction with the Moser Jumpoff Road, where there is more space for parking).

The ride:

0.0 Pedal east on gravel Moser Creek Road; begin moderate climb.

0.6 Road forks. Go left on Moser Jumpoff Road (FR 3159).

1.4 Watch for spur and gated closure on right, signed for Bozeman (Sourdough) Creek. Pass through gate and begin 2-mile downhill run on abandoned logging road that is reverting to singletrack.

2.4 Spur road on left; stay on main route straight ahead.

3.2 Slight uphill for 0.1 mile. At mile 4.5 the road swoops down into a glade of old trees and bottoms out in a hairpin turn to the left.

4.4 As the road comes out of the hairpin turn, just past a blue blaze (nailed on a tree), watch for singletrack coming in on the right. Turn right and begin moderate climb on broad switchbacks. Dense alder thickets close in on the trail, disguising this old logging road bed.

4.9 Grade eases slightly.

5.2 Small stream crossing; may be boggy.

5.7 Turn right and uphill off road bed onto singletrack. Trail climbs steeply 0.3 mile to ridgetop clearcut.

6.0 Top of climb (6,820 feet); bear left.

6.1 Spur goes right; stay to left and descend rutted, bumpy hillside.

6.3 Rejoin Moser Creek Road. Go right here if you've had enough—it's 0.9 mile downhill to the Moser-Jumpoff junction (see mile 0.6 above) and the return leg to your car, making an 8.1-mile loop. Or go left and uphill to complete the Hyalite Challenge race course.

7.0 Four-way junction and end of climb on Moser Creek Road (6,855 feet). Go straight (downhill) on main road.

7.2 Road bottoms out in a sharp right-hand turn. Ignore the doubletrack that drops right from the road. Instead, pedal 50 yards and watch for a singletrack over a kelly hump on the right. This trail drops for 1.4 miles, following an old logging track broken by frequent kelly humps and dips. CAUTION: Slow down for humps.

7.9 Sweeping right and left hairpin turns.

8.0 Spur track comes down from right; stay on main trail.

8.3 Singletrack goes right and uphill; stay on main trail, downhill.

8.6 Trail drops to fenceline; go right and up abrupt hill (ugh!). Continue 0.2-mile steady climb through meadow and then drop into trees.

8.9 Trail forks: go right to stay on official race course (left drops to Moser Creek Road).

9.0 Rejoin Moser Creek Road at fork with Moser Jumpoff Road. Turn left (downhill).

9.6 Junction with Hyalite Canyon Road.

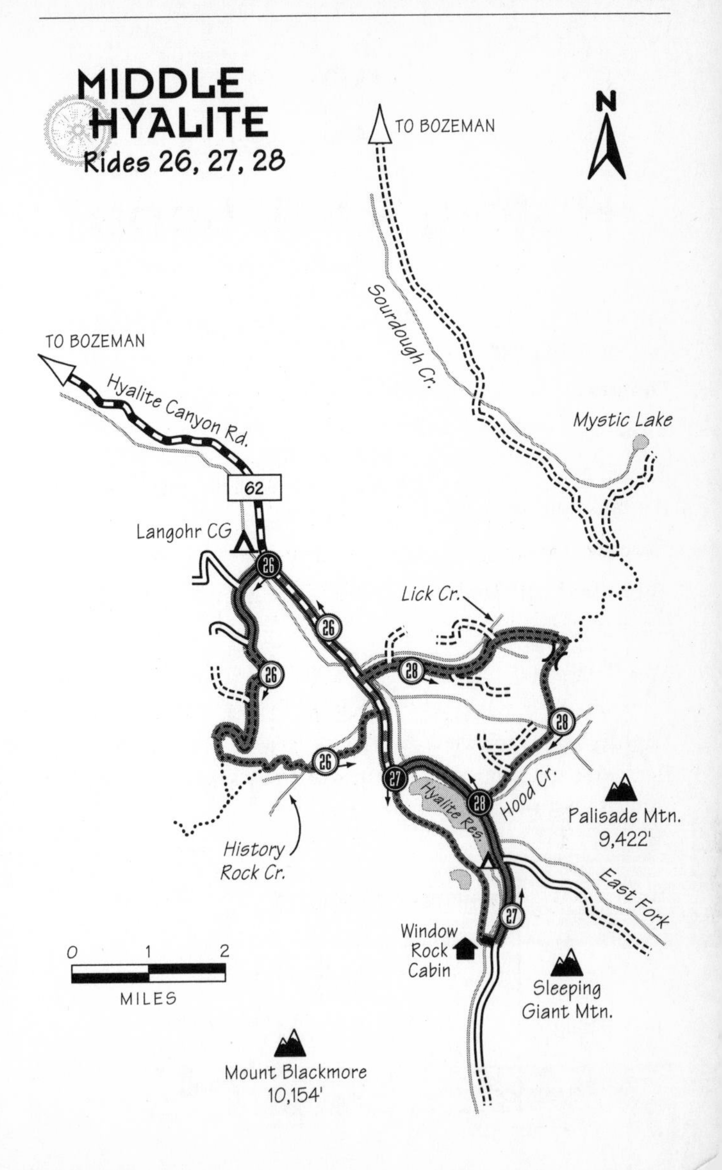
MIDDLE
HYALITE
Rides 26, 27, 28
TO BOZEMAN
N
Sourdough Cr.
TO BOZEMAN
Hyalite Canyon Rd.
Mystic Lake
62
Langohr CG
26
Lick Cr.
26
26
28
28
26
27
28
Hood Cr.
Hyalite Res.
Palisade Mtn.
9,422'
History
Rock Cr.
East Fork
27
Window
Rock
Cabin
0 1 2
MILES
Sleeping
Giant Mtn.
Mount Blackmore
10,154'

History Rock Loop

Location: 12 miles south of Bozeman in Hyalite Canyon. ***See map on page 101.***

Distance: 10.2-mile loop.

Time: 1 to 2 hours.

Tread: 4.6 miles on open logging road; 3 miles on singletrack; 2.6 miles on paved road.

Aerobic level: Moderate.

Technical difficulty: 1 on roads; 2 and some 3+ on singletrack.

Hazards: Traffic on Hyalite Canyon and Langohr roads; large, off-angle water bars on lower end of singletrack.

Highlights: Good views of Lower Hyalite drainage north to Bridgers; wildlife; and 3 miles of the sweetest, swoopiest singletrack in the region.

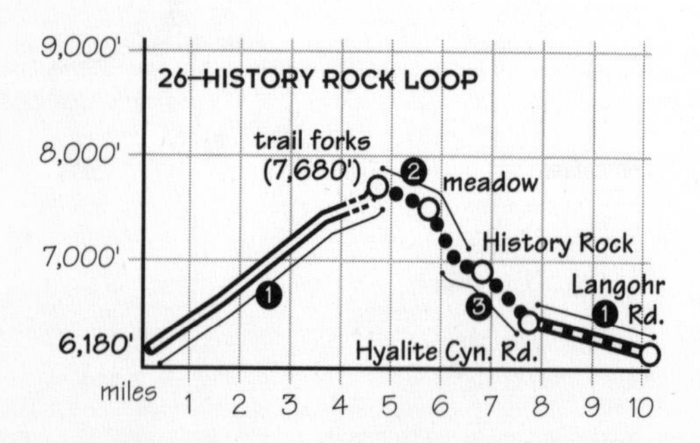

Land status: Gallatin National Forest.

Maps: Gallatin National Forest; USGS Wheeler Mountain, Mount Blackmore, Fridley Peak.

Access: From the corner of South 19th and Kagy Boulevard on the southwest edge of Bozeman, drive 6 miles south on South 19th. Turn left on paved Hyalite Canyon Road (FR 62) and drive 6.4 miles south to Langohr Road (FR 1046) on the right (0.4 mile past Langohr Campground). Turn onto Langohr Road and drop to the bridge over Hyalite Creek. Park in any of the numerous pullouts here.

The ride:

0.0 Langohr Road and bridge over Hyalite Creek. Pedal south up the main, gravel Langohr Road.

0.3 Spur road on right; stay on main road straight ahead.

0.6 Langohr Tool Road on right; stay straight.

1.4 Langohr Fork Road on right then spur on left; stay straight.

1.5 Enjoy brief downhill and easy grade—it's the only real break on this long climb.

1.8 Resume moderate climb.

2.4 Hairpin turn to left. Good views of the lower Hyalite drainage and north to the Bridgers.

3.4 Grade eases slightly.

3.5 Spur road on right; stay left.

3.6 Resume moderate climb along base of clearcut. The road narrows and switchbacks through the clearcut, with more good views north.

4.5 Pedal onto small saddle on ridge. A spur goes right; turn left. A sign points to History Rock Trail 424—a rough jeep track that climbs a short but steep hill. This doubletrack then breaks downhill and right; stay left on singletrack and skirt the upper edge of the clearcut.

4.6 Trail forks (7,680 feet). CAUTION: The left-hand fork—the one we're looking for—is all but invisible. A Forest Service sign is sometimes in place. If not, the main trail appears to go right, marked by prominent orange blazes leading into the trees. Instead, go left along edge of clearcut—the trail may be faint at first but soon becomes obvious. (Trials riders and endorphin junkies may enjoy a detour on the right-hand fork. It climbs a 0.5-mile slippery root staircase (5+!) to a windswept meadow above upper Cottonwood Creek with stunning views of 10,154-foot Mount Blackmore—a great picnic spot!)

4.8 Trail re-enters trees and skirts the upper edge of the clearcut.

5.6 Lean right and away from clearcut.

5.7 Enter meadow with view east to Hyalite Reservoir. The trail cuts across the meadow and drops into the first of 6 switchbacks, all snug but fun to ride. The root wads from blown-down trees add minor whoop-de-doos to the fun. As the trail eases down into the lush forest along the bottom of History Rock Creek, watch for deer, elk, and moose.

6.2 Final switchback; trail snakes through a long streambottom meadow. Sections here are heavily overgrown and the trail is trenched in places; keep your speed in check.

6.5 Short boggy spot.

6.7 History Rock. Pioneers carved their names in this rock back in the 1800s. From here the trail widens and water bars are numerous. Expect other trail users, especially on weekends.

7.4 Switchback right and onto an old logging road; bear right.
7.5 Trail crosses meadow on gravel corduroy; yield to other trail users.
7.6 History Rock trailhead and parking lot. Turn left on Hyalite Canyon Road.
10.2 Turn left onto Langohr Road (FR 1046) and pedal to your vehicle.

Hyalite Reservoir Loop

Location: 14 miles south of Bozeman at the north end of the Gallatin Range. ***See map on page 101.***

Distance: 6.2-mile loop.

Time: 45 minutes to 1.5 hours.

Tread: 3.6 miles on gravel roads; 2.6 miles on singletrack.

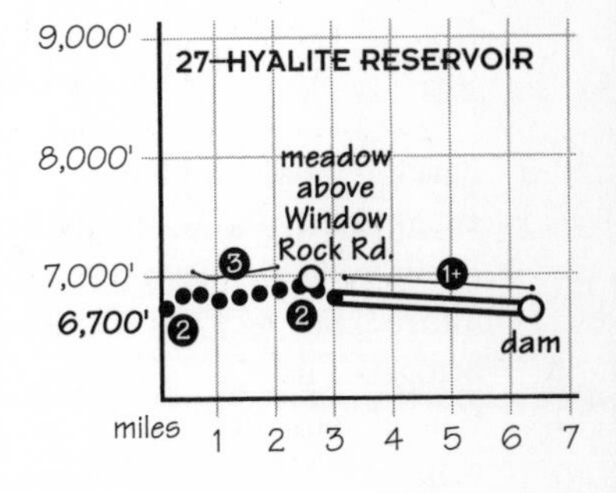

Aerobic level: Mostly easy with 5 or 6 strenuous but short climbs on the singletrack leg.

Technical difficulty: 1 to 2; some short sections of 3+ on singletrack.

Hazards: Watch for traffic on gravel roads; fat, off-angled water bars on West Shore Trail may cause falls.

Highlights: West Shore Trail is ugly (lots of logging debris) but fun, a good test piece for novice and intermediate riders; views of Hyalite Reservoir; spectacular views of the peaks along the West Fork of Hyalite Creek.

Land status: Gallatin National Forest.

Maps: Gallatin National Forest; USGS Fridley Peak.

Access: From the corner of South 19th and Kagy Boulevard on the southwest edge of Bozeman, drive 6 miles south on South 19th. Turn left on paved Hyalite Canyon Road (FR 62) and drive 10.2 miles south to Hyalite Reservoir (the pavement ends at 10 miles). On the northwest corner of the reservoir (before crossing the dam) turn right into the large parking lot and trailhead for Blackmore and West Shore trails.

The ride:

0.0 Parking lot and trailhead. A map of local trails is posted at the south end of the parking lot near the outhouse. From here, pedal south on the wide gravel trail (West Shore Trail 431) and immediately cross a wooden bridge.

0.1 Gravel path bends left. Go straight onto wide, dirt singletrack.

0.2 Junction with Crescent Lake Trail 213 (an optional route, but it's steep and highly technical) on right. Bear left to stay on the West Shore Trail.

0.3 Shore access trail drops to the left. Bank right and begin a moderate climb through two broad switchbacks.

0.5 Top of climb (about 6,800 feet) followed by 0.1-mile descent. CAUTION: Watch for big, off-angled water bars.

1.0 Next 0.6 mile features frequent steep but short climbs and drops. More fat water bars.

1.6 Rejoin Crescent Lake Trail 213. Bear left along east shore of pond.

1.9 Enter meadows at head of Hyalite Reservoir. Follow wooden posts if trail is overgrown. Two small stream crossings may be boggy until mid July.

2.0 Re-enter forest and stomp into a short, rocky climb (probably the most technical section of the ride—but it's do-able). Enjoy the next stretch of smooth, fast singletrack.

2.4 Enter meadows (about 6,800 feet) full of wildflowers, with Window Rock, Sleeping Giant, and the Hyalite peaks rising on all sides.

2.6 Trail drops onto the Window Rock Cabin access road. Turn left and cross the bridge over the West Fork of Hyalite Creek.

2.7 Pass around gate on left side and then lean left on the access road to...

2.8 The West Fork Road. CAUTION: Watch for traffic and turn left to complete the loop.

4.4 Junction with the East Fork Road on right. Go straight and pedal around the east shore of Hyalite Reservoir and across the dam on the main gravel road.

6.2 Parking lot and trailhead.

Lick Creek – Hood Creek Loop

Location: 12 miles south of Bozeman, or 1.5 miles north of Hyalite Reservoir, on the divide between Hyalite and Sourdough (Bozeman) creeks. ***See map on page 101.***

Distance: 9.8 miles.

Time: 1 to 2 hours.

Tread: 1.4 miles gravel road; 1.4 miles paved road; 3.7 miles old logging road; 3.3 miles singletrack.

Aerobic level: Mostly moderate with several short strenuous sections.

Technical difficulty: 1-2 for roaded sections; singletrack is mostly 3 with spots of 4. Last 0.5 mile is 4.

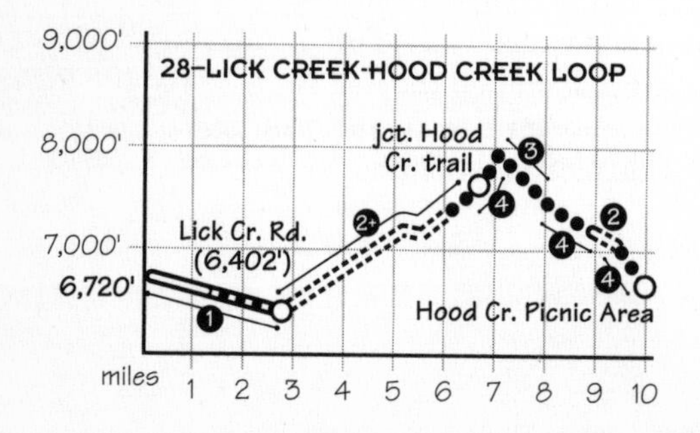

Hazards: Watch for traffic on Hyalite Road, especially at ride's end when entering road from steep trail. Lick Creek Road has frequent kelly humps (large dirt mounds across route).

Highlights: Great views of Hyalite Reservoir and surrounding mountains; 3.3 miles of fun and sometimes challenging singletrack; fairly low use.

Land status: Gallatin National Forest.

Maps: Gallatin National Forest; USGS Mount Ellis, Fridley Peak.

Access: From the corner of South 19th and Kagy Boulevard on the southwest edge of Bozeman, drive 6 miles south on South 19th. Turn left (south) on paved Hyalite Canyon Road (FR 62) and drive 10.2 miles (pavement ends at 10 miles) to Hyalite Reservoir (note gated Lick Creek Road on the left at 8.6 miles). At the reservoir, drive across the dam and go another 1.2 miles to Hood Creek boat ramp and picnic area on the right (about 0.6 mile past Hood Creek Campground). Go down the access road and take the first left. Day-use visitors can avoid the overnight camping fee by parking at sites 19 (by the outhouse) or 20.

The ride:

0.0 From the picnic area pedal back up to the main road. Look right 50 feet to see where Hood Creek Trail 436 comes out—the end of this ride. Turn left and pedal back across the dam and zip down Hyalite Road.

2.7 Turn right onto Lick Creek Road (about 0.5 mile downhill from History Rock Trailhead). Go around the bar gate and start climbing.

2.9 Wire cattle gate; close it behind you. Road climbs steadily through old clearcuts. Frequent kelly humps.

4.5 Spur road goes left; stay straight. Grade eases slightly.
5.1 Road comes into clearcut hillside. Ignore the foreground and enjoy spectacular views of Mount Blackmore, Sleeping Giant Mountain, and Hyalite Peak.
5.2 Fast descent for 0.3 mile. CAUTION: Slow down for two kelly humps.
5.5 Begin 0.2-mile strenuous climb.
6.2 Yet another clearcut; four rough and muddy kelly humps. Road becomes a skidder track.
6.5 Singletrack veers right and uphill into stump farm.
6.6 Trail tops out on Lick Creek/Bozeman Creek divide at 7,700 feet then drops slightly to...
6.7 Junction with Hood Creek Trail 436. Delusional downhillers can go left to drop 1,300 feet in about 1.5 miles (killer switchbacks!), then another 3 miles to the Sourdough Creek Road (see Ride 20). The rest of us go right along the divide ridge.
6.9 Trail drops back into forest.
7.1 Several short, steep climbs.
7.6 Trail turns sharply right and drops to a boggy stream crossing. CAUTION: steep, loose slope; better to dismount and walk down to stream. Cross on log.
7.9 Trail enters old, recovering clearcut; frequent water bars and abrupt dips in trail.
8.0 Corduroy bridge over stream.
8.1 Singletrack on old logging roadbed. Veer left and uphill to stay on trail.
8.4 Begin long descent on open ridge. Upper section offers great views of Hyalite Reservoir and Mount Blackmore—on a breezy, sun-filled day you can hear Julie Andrews singing "The hills are aliiiiive." Lower section is loose and rocky with several off-angled water bars.

9.2 Sharp but rideable switchback to left; trail drops onto old logging road. Go straight (south).
9.3 Trail drops to the right off logging road into clearcut. Begin rough (level 4) 0.5-mile descent with some off-the-seat steeps, loose rocks, and water bars.
9.7 Trail cuts straight across logging road.
9.8 Steep drop onto Hyalite Road. CAUTION: Watch for traffic. Turn right and go 50 feet to Hood Creek picnic area.

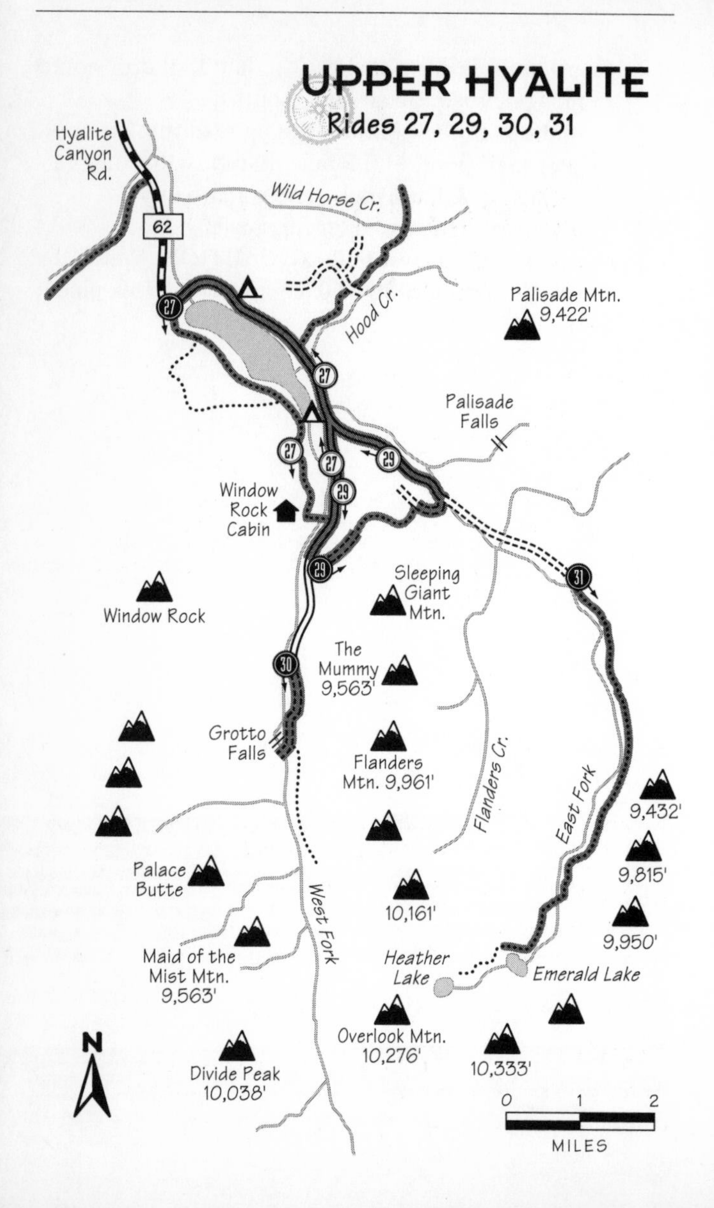
UPPER HYALITE
Rides 27, 29, 30, 31
Hyalite Canyon Rd.
62
Wild Horse Cr.
Hood Cr.
Palisade Mtn. 9,422'
Palisade Falls
Window Rock Cabin
Sleeping Giant Mtn.
Window Rock
The Mummy 9,563'
Grotto Falls
Flanders Mtn. 9,961'
Flanders Cr.
East Fork
9,432'
9,815'
9,950'
Palace Butte
West Fork
10,161'
Maid of the Mist Mtn. 9,563'
Heather Lake
Emerald Lake
Overlook Mtn. 10,276'
10,333'
Divide Peak 10,038'
N
0 1 2
MILES

Sleeping Giant Scramble

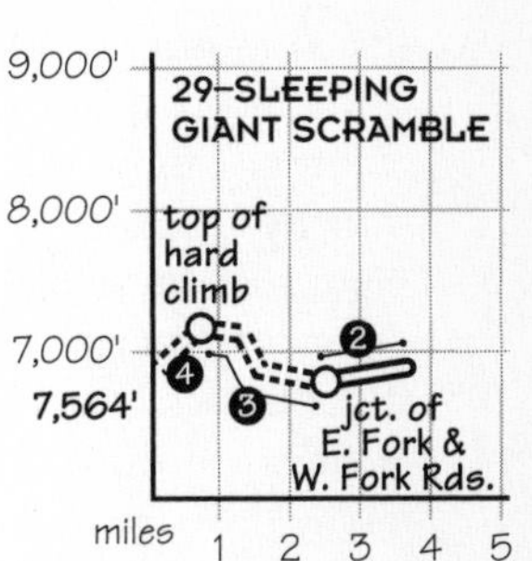

Location: 15 miles south of Bozeman, near the southeast end of Hyalite Reservoir.

Distance: 3.6-mile loop.

Time: 30 minutes to 1 hour.

Tread: 2.1 miles on gravel roads; 1.1 miles on doubletrack; 0.4 mile on singletrack.

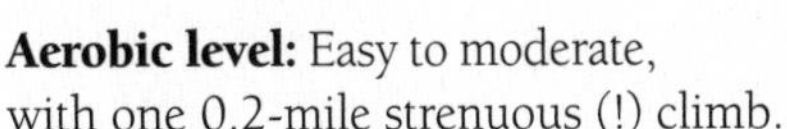

Aerobic level: Easy to moderate, with one 0.2-mile strenuous (!) climb.

Technical difficulty: 1 on roads; 2 on doubletrack; 3 to 4 on singletrack.

Hazards: Watch for traffic on East Fork and West Fork roads; trail may be hard to follow through clearcut.

Highlights: A "remote" scramble over the foot of Sleeping Giant Mountain; light use; a good loop to tie in with Hyalite Reservoir or Lick Creek loops (see rides 27 and 28).

Land status: Gallatin National Forest; Big Sky Lumber.

Maps: Gallatin National Forest; USGS Fridley Peak.

Access: From the corner of South 19th and Kagy Boulevard on the southwest edge of Bozeman, drive 6 miles south on South

19th. Turn left (south) on paved Hyalite Canyon Road (FR 62) and drive 10.2 miles (pavement ends at 10 miles) to Hyalite Reservoir. Drive across the dam and go another 1.8 miles. Bear right where the East Fork Road splits to the left and drive 1.3 miles on the West Fork Road to an unmarked parking pullout on the left.

The ride:

0.0 Parking pullout and trailhead on West Fork Road. Pedal north over two "whoa-Nelly!" kelly humps and contour east on old logging road doubletrack through brushy clearcuts.
0.2 Spur road on right; stay on main track straight ahead.
0.3 Spur road on right; stay straight.
0.5 Doubletrack grows faint and begins hard climb. Aim for a smear-of-dirt singletrack that goes straight uphill along the edge of the clearcut.
0.7 Top of hard climb (about 7,240 feet). Look east (left) for a blue cross-country ski blaze nailed to a tree. The trail enters a narrow corridor through the trees here; rooty but passable.
0.9 Pedal through a shallow stream crossing and into a small meadow. Follow doubletrack northeast into trees and downhill. CAUTION: Stay on the left track and watch for deep ruts. Ignore all spur roads and lean downhill.
1.3 Junction with another old logging road. Turn right (downhill).
1.5 Hairpin turn to left to East Fork Road. Go left (north). It's downhill all the way to...
2.3 Junction with Hyalite Road. Turn left onto the West Fork Road.
3.6 Parking pullout and trailhead on left.

Grotto Falls

Location: 16 miles south of Bozeman and south of Hyalite Reservoir, along the West Fork of Hyalite Creek. ***See map on page 112.***

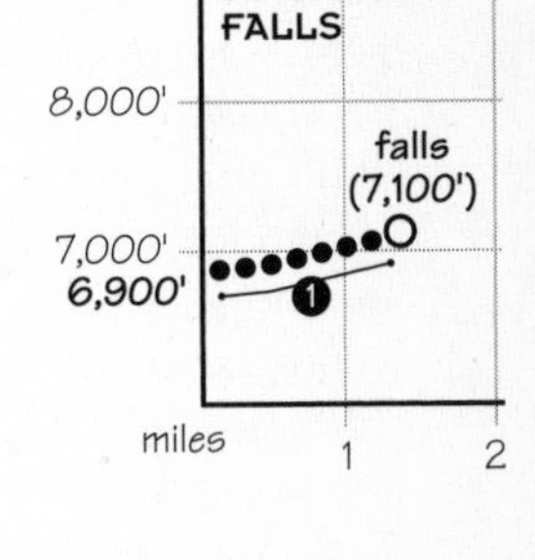

Distance: 2.3 miles round trip.

Time: 15 to 25 minutes (plus time to dangle your toes in the stream).

Tread: Wide, two-way, gravel, barrier-free trail.

Aerobic level: Easy.

Technical difficulty: 1.

Hazards: Watch for folks in wheelchairs, bikes, horses, kids, dogs, lungfish, and the Jamaican bobsled team. Please ride slowly and in control at all times.

Highlights: An easy, shaded ride to a beautiful waterfall.

Land status: Gallatin National Forest.

Maps: USGS Fridley Peak.

Access: From the corner of South 19th and Kagy Boulevard on the southwest edge of Bozeman, drive 6 miles south on South 19th. Turn left (south) on paved Hyalite Canyon Road (FR 62) and drive 10.2 miles (pavement ends at 10 miles) to Hyalite Reservoir. Continue across the dam and along the east shore 1.8 miles. Bear right where the East Fork Road splits to the left and drive 2.8 miles on the West Fork Road to the parking lot and trailhead at road's end.

The ride:

0.0 Parking lot and trailhead. Pedal south on the wide jeep track.

0.2 Trail forks. Take the gravel Grotto Falls Trail up and to the left. This barrier-free trail gradually switchbacks across the old Hyalite Creek Trail as the two climb toward Grotto Falls. More intrepid riders can test their skills on the rocky, dirt Hyalite Creek Trail. CAUTION: Watch for other trail users, especially at frequent trail crossings.

1.1 Grade eases; picnic table on right. Lean right and pedal 150 yards to a bench overlooking Grotto Falls. Dismount and walk the final 100 feet to the base of the falls. Return to the trailhead by the same route. CAUTION: Please ride slowly on the descent. Skidding and disregard for other trail users will result in restrictions or loss of access for cyclists!

Emerald Lake

Location: 17 miles southeast of Bozeman, about 4 miles south of Hyalite Reservoir in the Hyalite Peaks high country.
See map on page 112.

Distance: 9 miles up and back.

Time: 2 to 3 hours.

Tread: Outrageous singletrack.

Aerobic level: Moderate to strenuous.

Technical difficulty: Mostly 3+ to 4, with a few spots of 5.

Hazards: Yield to other trail users. Pack a wind- and waterproof jacket—storms appear suddenly in this alpine world, typically bringing rain, sleet, or snow and plummeting temperatures. Yes, snow is possible, even in mid-July.

Highlights: This is the singletrack stairway to heaven. It has roots, rocks, and water bars, but always offers a rideable line. Intermediate riders will enjoy looping through the many switchbacks, all relatively easy to ride, up and down. Plus you get a babbling creek, wildlife, spectacular alpine scenery, and a "gem" of a lake.

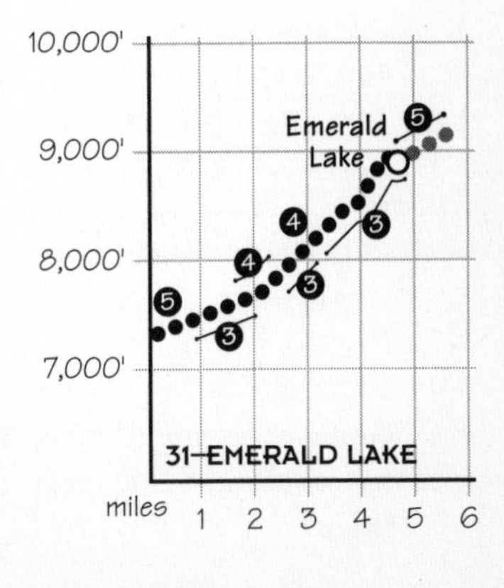

Land status: Gallatin National Forest.

Maps: Gallatin National Forest; USGS Fridley Peak.

Access: From the corner of South 19th and Kagy Boulevard on the southwest edge of Bozeman, drive 6 miles south on South 19th. Turn left (south) on paved Hyalite Canyon Road (FR 62) and drive 10.2 miles (pavement ends at 10 miles) to Hyalite Reservoir. Drive across the dam and go another 1.8 miles to a fork in the road. Go left on the East Fork Road (signed for Palisade Falls) and drive 1.7 miles to the Palisade Falls picnic area on the left. Bear right here and continue 1.2 miles to the Emerald Lake trailhead and parking lot at road's end.

The ride:

0.0 Parking lot and trailhead. Pedal south on the wide, well-used Trail 434 as it heads into the forest. Don't be discouraged by the initial rocky sections—they're about the worst this trail dishes up.

0.5 Low wooden bridge over a side stream.

0.9 Loop left then right through two easy, open switchbacks.

2.0 0.1-mile strenuous climb, a 4 for difficulty due to loose and fixed rocks.

2.2 Two easy, open switchbacks.

2.4 Stream crossing.

2.9 Stream crossing. Begin strenuous climb through first long series of switchbacks.

3.5 Grade eases.

3.7 Drop to another stream crossing.

3.9 Begin second set of switchbacks and strenuous climb.

4.4 Grade eases slightly (but there's no oxygen at this altitude—about 8,900 feet). Terrific views of surrounding ridges.

4.5 Trail drops easily to north shore of Emerald Lake. Lakeshore trail splits left. Right goes around west shore of lake and then climbs hard (!) over sections of 5+ terrain 0.9 mile to Heather Lake. Cyclists, let's show some restraint and leave the trail to Heather for hikers and solitary souls. After soaking up the breath-taking scenery, return to the trailhead by retracing your tracks. Please stay on the designated trail—do not cut switchbacks—and ride in control so you can yield to other trail users.

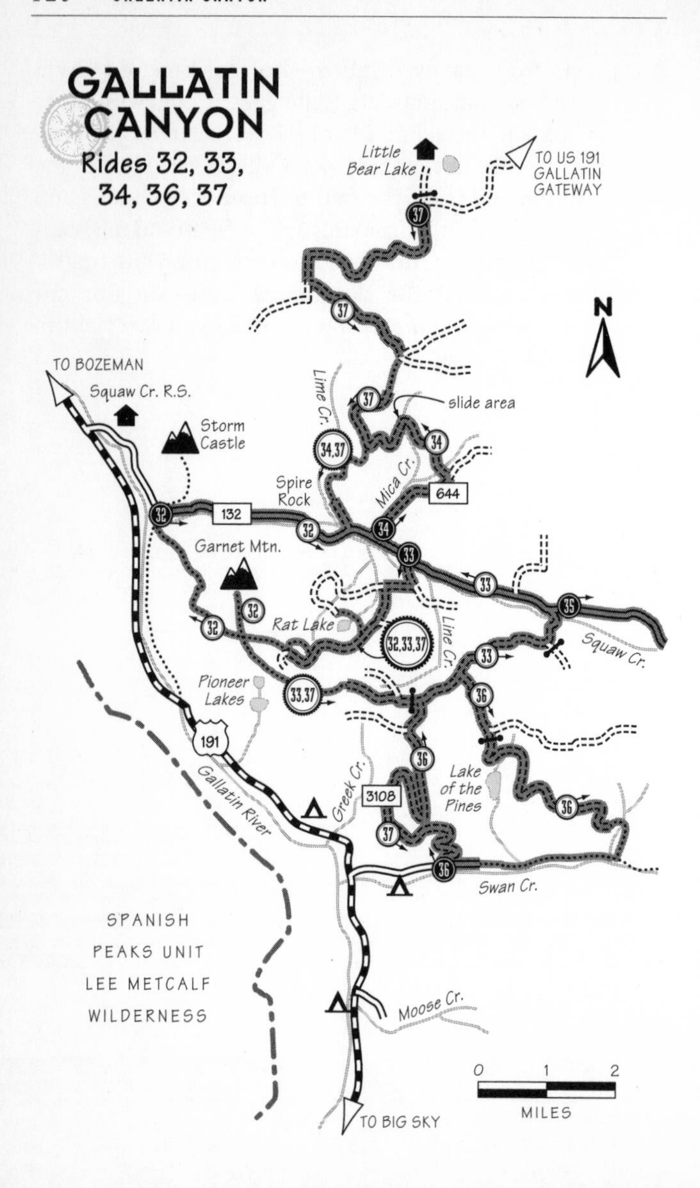

GALLATIN CANYON
Rides 32, 33, 34, 36, 37
Little Bear Lake
TO US 191 GALLATIN GATEWAY
N
TO BOZEMAN
Squaw Cr. R.S.
Storm Castle
Lime Cr.
slide area
Spire Rock
Mica Cr.
644
132
Garnet Mtn.
Rat Lake
Lime Cr.
Squaw Cr.
Pioneer Lakes
191
Gallatin River
Greek Cr.
3108
Lake of the Pines
Swan Cr.
SPANISH PEAKS UNIT LEE METCALF WILDERNESS
Moose Cr.
0 1 2
MILES
TO BIG SKY

Garnet Mountain Loop

Location: 17 miles south of Bozeman, in the Squaw Creek drainage on the east side of Gallatin Canyon.

Distance: 13.1-mile loop.

Time: 2 to 3 hours.

Tread: 5 miles on open logging road; 1.8 miles on old, closed logging road; 3.1 miles on ATV doubletrack; and 3.2 miles on singletrack.

Aerobic level: Strenuous.

Technical difficulty: 2 on roads; 3 to 4 on double- and singletrack.

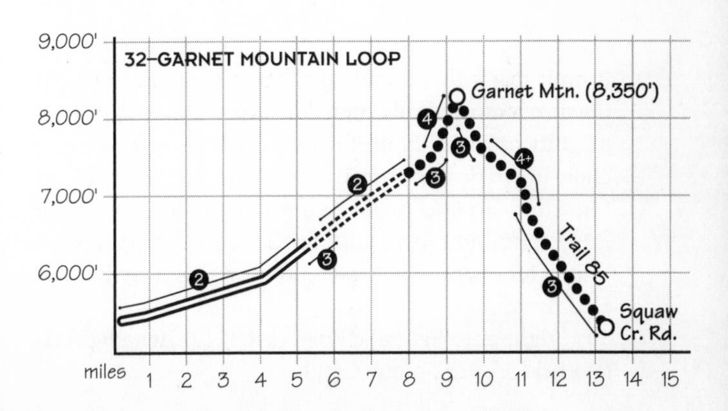

Hazards: Watch for traffic on Squaw Creek and Rat Lake roads. Stay off exposed ridges and Garnet Mountain summit if lightning storms are likely. Sections of Garnet Mountain Trail 85 are extremely narrow, cutting across dangerously steep slopes with severe exposure—wandering off trail here could be fatal.

Highlights: Rat Lake; a terrific hillclimb workout; stupendous 360-degree views from Garnet Mountain Lookout; 3.2 miles of heart-in-your-mouth (but still fun) singletrack.

Land status: Gallatin National Forest.

Maps: Gallatin National Forest; USGS Garnet Mountain.

Access: From Bozeman drive 9 miles west on MT 84 to Four Corners. Turn left and drive 17.3 miles south on US 191. Turn left at the sign for the Squaw Creek Ranger Station and cross the bridge over the Gallatin River. Turn right onto gravel Squaw Creek Road (FR 132) and drive 1.9 miles south and east. About 100 yards past the church camp on the right look for the trailhead signs for Gallatin River Trail 137 and Garnet Mountain Trail 85, also on the right. Park here, pulling well off the road.

The ride:

0.0 Rumor has it that a few Bozeman bikers have tackled the unrelenting climb offered by Garnet Mountain Trail 85. But most folks prefer the route described here, choosing to descend via Trail 85. So, turn your back on the trailhead and pedal east on gravel Squaw Creek Road, climbing gradually for 3.7 miles. CAUTION: Watch for traffic and loose gravel on this heavily traveled route.

3.7 Turn right onto Rat Lake Road (FR 3112), which drops to a bridge over Squaw Creek.

4.0 Lean right (a spur road goes left) and uphill. Begin a moderate but well-shaded climb.

4.6 Spur goes right; stay left (signed for Rat Lake, 1 mile).

5.0 The road makes a big hairpin left. At the apex of the turn take the signed trail on the right over the kelly hump. This wide, rocky route is heavily used by ATVers.

5.3 Old slide area. Take the narrow singletrack on the uphill side through the slide. Shortly after this, a singletrack splits off right—a steep "shortcut" to the road to Rat Lake. Instead, stay straight on the main route.

5.4 Turn left on old (closed) logging road. Right goes 0.1 mile to the shores of Rat Lake (prettier than its name and worth the detour). An unofficial ATV route climbs from the lake's northwest shore, but it's plagued by erosion. Plans are to close it. The logging road climbs moderately through trees above the Rat Lake basin, winding west then north.

7.1 ATV doubletrack goes right, marked by a wooden post. Stay on the road for more moderate climbing.

7.8 Now we can follow the ATV track, which veers right, off the old roadbed. It scampers up a strenuous, loose rocky climb.

8.0 Grade eases; brief downhill to clearing.

8.1 Resume moderately strenuous climb; some rutted sections.

8.4 Near the top of the ridge, watch for the trail sign for Pioneer Lakes Trail 79 on the left (see Ride 27). Lean right here and continue climbing.

8.5 Garnet Mountain Trail 85 drops away on left. For the 15-minute strenuous climb to the summit of Garnet Mountain, stay right and keep climbing on the loose, rocky ATV doubletrack. The track follows crude switchbacks, sometimes attacking the fall line directly. The toughest pitch is about one-third of the way up from the junction with Trail 85. The air may seem thinner toward the summit, but the trail's grade actually eases as it climbs through grassy meadows to...

9.2 Garnet Mountain Lookout (8,350 feet). This old fire lookout can be rented from the Bozeman Ranger District of the Gallatin National Forest. Day visitors can bask in the breeze on the lookout's deck, enjoying outstanding 360-degree views. Look west to Lava Lake, 10,416-foot Jumbo Mountain, and other high summits in the Spanish Peaks. Turn north to see the Tobacco Root, Elkhorn, and Big Belt mountains rimming the horizon. The Bridger Range ripples against the sky on the northeast, leading into the Hyalite Peaks and the Gallatin Crest crowding the east and south vista. Return to Trail 85 by retracing your tread down the main summit trail.

9.9 Watch for the trail sign (the trail itself is hard to see on descent) and turn right onto Trail 85. It quickly bends north and contours onto steep (!) open slopes. CAUTION: The tread here is narrow, falls away with the slope, and is loose in spots. The downhill side is steep, sometimes almost vertical. A fall or simply riding off the edge of the trail will result in serious injury or death. Ride in control or dismount on the uphill side and walk your bike.

10.6 End of steep exposure; trail enters a meadow.

10.9 Re-enter trees.

11.1 Sharp (!) switchback right; dense undergrowth crowds the trail.

11.4 Several more sharp switchbacks with some short, steep drops in between.

12.0 Awkward, rocky drop and turn right with cliff straight

ahead. Most folks should dismount and walk until trail clears this small rock outcrop. The tread is smooth and stays closer to Earth—a welcome relief—from here on out. But keep an eye ahead for other users and downfall on the trail.

12.8 Gallatin River Trail 137 comes in on left; stay straight.

13.1 Cross the wooden bridge over Squaw Creek to your car on the main road.

Rat Lake Loop

Location: 15 miles south of Bozeman in Gallatin Canyon up the Squaw Creek drainage. ***See map on page 120.***

Distance: 13.6

Time: 1.5 to 2.5 hours.

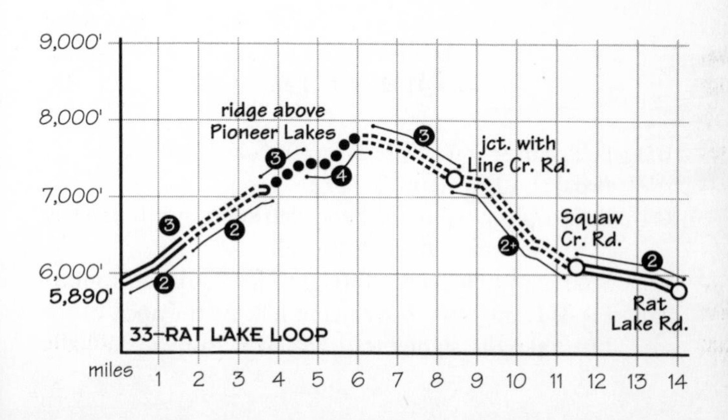

Tread: 6.5 miles on open logging roads; 4.4 miles on closed logging road; 2.7 miles on ATV doubletrack.

Aerobic level: Moderate with a handful of strenuous climbs.

Technical difficulty: 2 on logging roads; 3 to 4 on doubletrack.

Hazards: Watch for traffic on open roads. Ride in control on the Line Creek Road descent—there are sharp turns with sheer dropoffs. Also steep dropoffs to the right (west) of trail above Pioneer Lakes.

Highlights: Rat Lake; aerial views of Pioneer Lakes; sections of fun, ATV-width trail.

Land status: Gallatin National Forest; Big Sky Lumber.

Maps: Gallatin National Forest; USGS Garnet Mountain.

Access: From Bozeman drive 9 miles west on MT 84 to Four Corners. Turn left and drive 17.3 miles south on US 191. Turn left at the sign for the Squaw Creek Ranger Station and cross the bridge over the Gallatin River. Turn right onto gravel Squaw Creek Road (FR 132) and drive 5.7 miles south and east. Turn right on Rat Lake Road (FR 3112) and park in one of the many informal camping/picnic sites on either side of the bridge over Squaw Creek.

The ride:

0.0 Bridge over Squaw Creek on Rat Lake Road (FR 3112). Pedal southwest on FR 3112.

0.1 Lean right (a spur road goes left) and uphill. Begin a moderate but well-shaded climb.

0.7 Spur goes right; stay left (signed for Rat Lake, 1 mile).

1.1 FR 3112 makes a big hairpin left. At the apex of the turn take the signed trail on the right over the kelly hump. This wide, rocky route is heavily used by ATVers.

1.4 Old slide area. Take the narrow singletrack on the uphill side through the slide. Shortly after this, a singletrack splits off right—a steep "shortcut" to the road to Rat Lake. Instead, stay straight on the main route.

1.5 Turn left on old (closed) logging road. Right goes 0.1 mile to the shores of Rat Lake (prettier than its name and worth the detour). An unofficial ATV route climbs from the lake's northwest shore, but it's plagued by erosion. Plans are to close it. The logging road climbs moderately through trees above the Rat Lake basin, winding west then north.

3.2 ATV doubletrack goes right, marked by a wooden post. Stay on the road for more moderate climbing.

3.9 Now we can follow the ATV track, which veers right, off the old roadbed. It scampers up a strenuous, loose rocky climb.

4.1 Grade eases; brief downhill to clearing.

4.2 Resume moderately strenuous climb; some rutted sections.

4.5 Near the top of the ridge, turn left at the sign for Pioneer Lakes Trail 79. (Or detour right and uphill (!) to the summit of Garnet Mountain—see Ride 27.) Going left, the ATV doubletrack drops through a patch of perennial downfall and then beelines southeast through a dense stand of lodgepole pine.

4.6 Boggy spot.

5.2 Climbing slightly the trail breaks out of the trees and onto an open ridge above Pioneer Lakes to the west. CAUTION: Steep dropoffs to the right of trail; dismount and walk to overlooks. Views extend west into the Spanish Peaks unit of the Lee Metcalf Wilderness.

The trail stays just left of the cliff here, rolling over small knobs and winding around clumps of fir.

5.4 Prominent point overlooking Pioneer Lakes.

5.5 Short, steep climb into trees.

5.7 Short drop. Trail then swings east and climbs into an old clearcut.

6.2 As views open up to the north and east, the track widens into an old, overgrown logging road. A wooden post (at about 7,700 feet) marks the route. From here the road makes a quick descent through young stands of pine.

6.9 The road cuts through a nondescript saddle between two low knobs. Continue the downhill run.

7.6 Another old logging road joins in from the left; lean right (check your speed before hitting this turn: it's slightly off-camber and tends to be loose and sandy). The road drops through more clearcuts, then levels off. Watch for boggy sections on the flats.

8.2 Gate and junction with Line Creek Road (FR 3108). Turn left and hang on for a wild downhill. The first mile isn't bad, but then the road gets rockier and twistier, with some sheer dropoffs on the outsides of turns. Ride in control.

8.9 Pine Tree Road goes right; stay straight on main road.

9.8 Sharp turn right; rough, rocky tread as road crosses old landslide.

10.4 Orchid Gulch Road (gated) on right; stay left on main road.

10.8 Hang on for three sharp hairpin turns.

11.1 Bridge over Squaw Creek.

11.2 Turn left on Squaw Creek Road (FR 132). This rough gravel road feels like a highway after Line Creek.

13.4 Watch for a dirt jeep track dropping sharply left down

to Rat Lake Road (if you miss it, just go another 50 yards to the official turn-off).

13.6 Bridge over Squaw Creek and parking area.

Mica Creek Loop

Location: 15 miles south of Bozeman in Gallatin Canyon, up the Squaw Creek drainage. ***See map on page 120.***

Distance: 8.3-mile loop.

Time: 1.5 to 2.5 hours.

Tread: 5.7 miles on logging road; 2.6 miles on double- and ATV-width singletrack.

Aerobic level: Moderate.

Technical difficulty: 2 on roads; 3 on double- and singletrack.

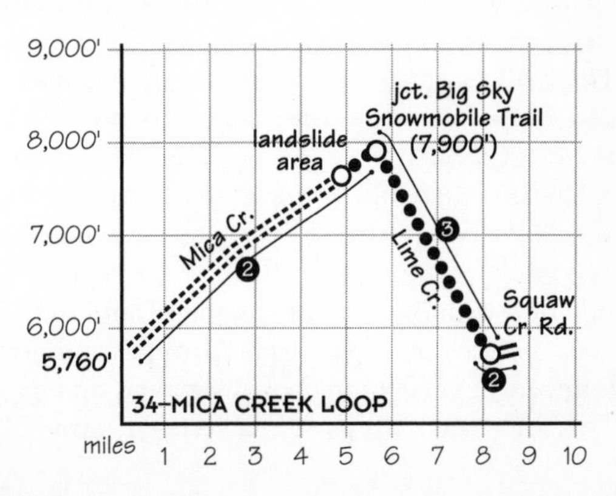

Hazards: Watch for traffic on roads, especially on Squaw Creek Road. Descent is loose and rocky in spots, with frequent water dips and sharp turns; ride in control.

Highlights: Not the most scenic, but one of the less strenuous climbs in Gallatin Canyon, and a fast, snaky descent through lush meadows along Lime Creek.

Land status: Gallatin National Forest.

Maps: Gallatin National Forest; USGS Garnet Mountain.

Access: From Bozeman drive 9 miles west on MT 84 to Four Corners. Turn left and drive 17.3 miles south on US 191. Turn left at the sign for the Squaw Creek Ranger Station and cross the bridge over the Gallatin River. Turn right onto gravel Squaw Creek Road (FR 132) and drive 5 miles south and east to Mica Creek Road (FR 644) on the left. Park off the road at this junction.

The ride:

0.0 From Squaw Creek Road, begin pedaling north up Mica Creek Road (FR 644) as it climbs moderately. The road switchbacks broadly, contouring across old, open clearcuts with little shade.

2.5 The road forks; go left, following orange blazes. The grade eases slightly as the road wraps around the head of Mica Creek.

4.7 A landslide here blocks travel to all but bikes, horses, and ATVs. Follow the ATV doubletrack across the slide. The grade beyond levels off.

5.4 Junction with Big Sky Snowmobile Trail (see Ride 32) and top of climb (7,900 feet). Turn left and downhill, following a yellow directional sign and orange blazes. This ATV track drops into a series of meadows and

Douglas-fir groves along Lime Creek, quickly losing elevation.

5.6 Bank right at snowmobile sign. Frequent water dips in trail—they help shed water but can also shake off fat tire flyers.

6.4 Lush meadows; watch for deer and other wildlife.

7.8 Fenceline and gate.

8.0 Squaw Creek Road; turn left and pedal east.

8.3 Mica Creek Road and parking.

Upper Squaw Creek

Location: 17 miles south of Bozeman in Gallatin Canyon, up the Squaw Creek drainage. ***See map on page 120.***

Distance: 11 (or more) miles up and back.

Time: 1 to 3 hours depending on total distance.

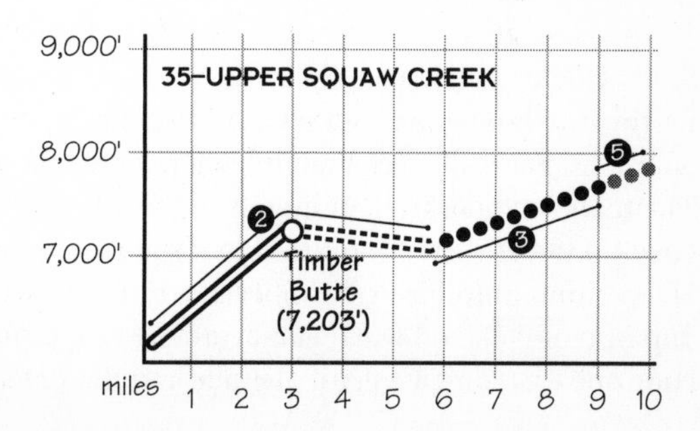

Tread: Logging road; wide packstock trail at upper end.

Aerobic level: On the easy end of moderate.

Technical difficulty: 2; 3 to 5+ on upper trail.

Hazards: Watch for traffic when road is open to motorized use. Also some sections of heavy gravel and loose rocks.

Highlights: A relatively easy road ride; fishing; chance of seeing deer, moose, and other wildlife.

Land status: Gallatin National Forest; Big Sky Lumber.

Maps: Gallatin National Forest; USGS Mount Blackmore, Garnet Mountain.

Access: From Bozeman drive 9 miles west on MT 84 to Four Corners. Turn left and drive 17.3 miles south on US 191. Turn left at the sign for the Squaw Creek Ranger Station and cross the bridge over the Gallatin River. Turn right onto gravel Squaw Creek Road (FR 132) and drive 7.9 miles south and east to the end of the year-round road. Park here, pulling well off the road. (A gate here bars motorized access (except snowmobiles) from January 1 through June 30. This is also the junction with Line Creek Road, which crosses Squaw Creek and goes south to Swan Creek Road; see rides 33 and 36)

The ride:

0.0 Seasonal closure gate on Squaw Creek Road. Pedal east up the one-lane gravel Squaw Creek Road.

1.4 Spur road goes left; stay straight. Begin moderate climb.

1.6 The road bends north, looping in and out of the Spring Creek draw. It then contours above Squaw Creek.

2.1 Steep climb onto base of Timber Butte.

2.8 Top of climb (7,203 feet); good turn-around point. Or continue east, down a gradual grade and then climbing again to rejoin the banks of Squaw Creek.

5.5 Road devolves into jeep track and then pack trail as it continues climbing toward Hyalite Divide. It's possible to dance through the boulder fields and suck air all the way to Hyalite Ridge, but that's work. Keep it fun and turn around, retracing your tread back down the main Squaw Creek Road.

Swan Creek Loop

Location: 20 miles south of Bozeman in Gallatin Canyon, up the Swan Creek drainage. ***See map on page 120.***

Distance: 14.4-mile loop.

Time: 2 to 3 hours.

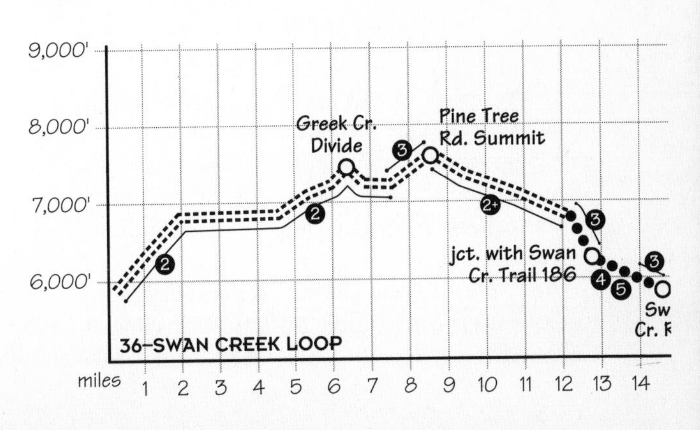

Tread: 8.5 miles on open logging road; 3.6 miles on closed logging road; 2.3 miles on singletrack.

Aerobic level: Moderate, with some strenuous climbing.

Technical difficulty: 2 on logging roads; 3 to 5+ and some unrideable sections on singletrack.

Hazards: Watch for (sparse) traffic on Line Creek Road; rough rocky sections on Swan Creek Trail 185.

Highlights: Very light use; good views from Line Creek Road; beautiful ride/walk along Swan Creek.

Land status: Gallatin National Forest; Big Sky Lumber.

Maps: Gallatin National Forest; USGS Mount Blackmore, Garnet Mountain.

Access: From Bozeman drive 9 miles west on MT 84 to Four Corners. Turn left and drive 25.4 miles south on US 191. Turn left at the sign for Swan Creek Campground (exactly 1 mile south of Greek Creek Campground on US 191). Drive 1.2 miles east on Swan Creek Road (FR 481), past the campground, to the small turn-around and junction with Line Creek Road (FR 3108) on the left. Park off the road here.

The ride:

0.0 From the cul-de-sac at the end of Swan Creek Road, pedal north up Line Creek Road (FR 3108). This one-lane logging road climbs steeply through broad hairpin turns, gaining about 800 feet in the first 1.5 miles. The lower sections are rocky and sandy, but the tread improves.

1.7 Grade levels off; frequent but short muddy spots.

2.0 Rocky outcrop overlook on left with views of the Gallatin Divide. Road bends north and enters a Douglas fir park-like clearcut.

3.4 Roadbed of logs for 50 yards.

3.7 Spur road goes left; stay on main road as it hairpins right and resumes climb.

4.4 Road hairpins left and climbs along base of cliffs and talus.

5.4 Spur goes right; stay left.

6.3 Sign marks Greek Creek Divide; top of climb (7,400 feet). A spur goes left; stay on main road and begin rutted descent into the Squaw Creek drainage.

6.7 Rat Lake Divide Road (FR 132-C) comes in on left (see Ride 28); lean right to stay on main road. Grade levels off.

7.4 Watch for a sign for Squaw Creek Road and a yellow merge sign. Turn right here, off the main road and onto Pine Tree Road, signed as a "primitive road not maintained for public travel." It climbs strenuously at first, then moderately for more than 0.7 mile on the lush north side of the ridge.

8.5 Pine Tree Road veers left (at about 7,620 feet); turn right onto a gated logging road (Lake of the Pines Road) and begin descending. Good views south, including the 10,095-foot peak at the head of Moose Creek.

9.1 Big hairpin left. From here the road snakes its way south and downhill through a near-treeless clearcut and then into the steep ravine above Lake of the Pines. Then it contours east, briefly in the trees, and resumes its drop toward Swan Creek.

12.0 Active logging area; bear right and downhill.

12.1 The road narrows here to ATV-width doubletrack and drops into the trees. It is well marked with many orange blazes.

12.5 Get off the seat for a 100-yard steep drop into a grassy bowl. Trail bends south.

12.6 Cross a small stream several times; boggy in places.
12.7 Junction with Swan Creek Trail 186. Ignore the blazes and directional arrows that lead left and across the stream. Instead, turn right and cross the tributary stream one last time. From here Trail 186 follows the north bank of Swan Creek downstream. Rideable sections are interspersed with level-5 or worse rock gardens for the next mile.
12.8 Short but steep rocky climb (a 4+ or 5).
13.0 Steep, rocky, cliff-side descent for 70 yards.
13.1 Another steep, rocky drop (5+).
13.2 Trail crosses a talus field.
13.3 Everybody get off and carry your bikes through 70 yards of boulders and old landslide debris.
13.7 Trail enters edge of beaver pond meadows. Trail is rocky but rideable.
13.9 Rough, rocky spot, then smooth again to the base of the beaver ponds.
14.0 Swan Creek Falls—where a slide blocked the stream. Trail dips and humps over old slide landscape and crosses a small side stream.
14.3 Tread widens to ATV-width gravel roadbed.
14.4 Swan Creek Road and parking area.

Little Bear to Swan Creek

Location: About 15 miles southwest of Bozeman in the ridges and valleys on the east side of Gallatin Canyon. ***See map on page 120.***

Distance: 25 miles, one way.

Time: 4 hours, but plan a full day to run the shuttle, ride, eat, snooze, and see the sights along the way.

Tread: 21.1 miles on logging road (5.6 miles of which are gated year-round); 3.9 miles on doubletrack or ATV-width singletrack.

Aerobic level: Strenuous (with some easy and moderate sections).

Technical difficulty: 2 on logging roads; 3 and 4 on doubletrack.

Hazards: Watch for traffic on open roads; yield to ATVs on open doubletrack. Save this ride for a sunny day; avoid exposed ridges during storms. Pack a jacket and plenty of food, water, and a repair kit.

Highlights: An epic journey over the rugged ridges of the north Gallatin Range; outstanding views of surrounding peaks; wildlife; Rat Lake; Pioneer Lakes; many opportunities for side trips.

Land status: Gallatin National Forest; Big Sky Lumber.

Maps: Gallatin National Forest; USGS Gallatin Gateway, Garnet Mountain.

Access: This ride requires a vehicle shuttle to leave a rig at trip's end at the Swan Creek Road cul-de-sac. From Bozeman drive 9 miles west on MT 84 (West Main or Huffine Lane) to Four Corners. Turn left and drive 25.4 miles south on US 191. Turn left at the sign for Swan Creek Campground (exactly 1 mile south of Greek Creek Campground on US 191). Drive 1.2 miles east on Swan Creek Road (FR 481), past the campground, to the small turn-around and junction with Line Creek Road (FR 3108) on the left. Park off the road here.

Now, to reach the start of the trip, drive back down to US 191. Turn right and drive north back through Gallatin Canyon almost all the way to Gallatin Gateway. At 17.3 miles from the Swan Creek Road (just before US 191 makes a big curve north to Gallatin Gateway), turn right (southeast) onto paved Little Bear Road. About 1.9 miles from US 191, Little Bear Road jogs right across a bridge; continue another 0.5 mile to pavement's end. From here the road becomes narrow and winding, with frequent blind curves.

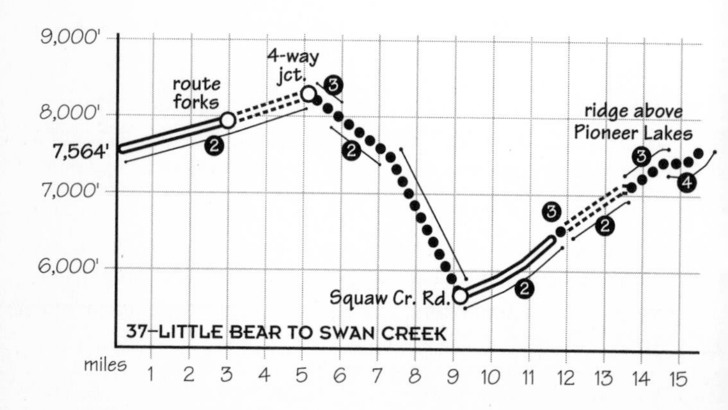

Stay on the main road as it works its way up the steep slope above Cliff Creek. At 8.2 miles from US 191 take the right-hand fork, signed as Wilson Creek Road (FR 3138). Follow this looping road west and south exactly 4 miles to the gated Little Bear Road (FR 6988) on the right. Park here, well off the road.

The ride:

0.0 Pedal west on the main road (FR 3138), keeping an eye out for traffic.

0.9 Gated spur road goes left; stay straight.

2.6 Spur road goes right; stay left.

2.9 The road forks. Veer left and uphill following orange blazes. About 30 feet up a sign posted on a tree points to Mica Creek. The road climbs along the 'dozer-scraped ridge, eventually leveling off as it winds south.

3.8 The road becomes a rough jeep track through an active logging clearcut. Stay on the main track, which remains fairly level.

5.1 A crossroads of sorts, with too many directional arrows and blazes. Take a hard right turn onto a well-traveled, ATV-width trail that drops into the trees. Orange metal blazes mark the route as the Big Sky Snowmobile Trail. This trail drops in a hurry, with some off-camber and sandy sections.

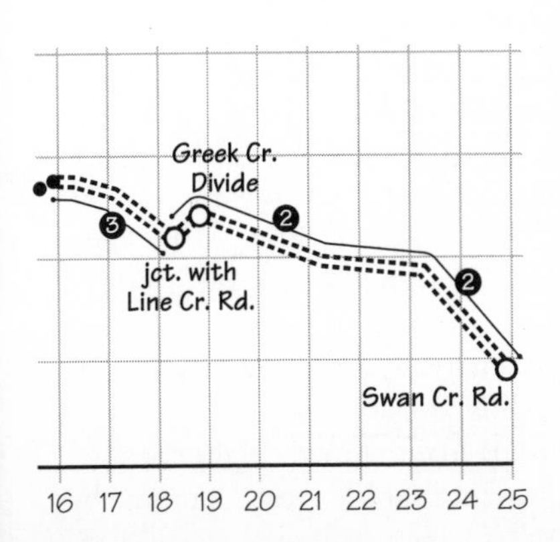

5.4 Trail enters an old clearcut with views across to the ridges above Gallatin Canyon. Follow the trail as it curves through the young crop of trees.

5.5 ATV trail drops onto old logging road grade and contours around a low ridge, dodging briefly back into a swatch of forest. The grade then wraps south around the head of Lime Creek, steadily losing elevation through another clearcut.

7.2 Slow down near a clump of trees and another odd crossroads. The logging road continues straight and a spur road goes left. But we'll follow the big arrow (and orange blazes) and bank into a hard right turn. Here the ATV track drops like a rope into a series of meadows and Douglas-fir groves along Lime Creek.

7.4 Bank right at snowmobile sign. Watch for frequent water dips in trail—they help shed water but can also shake off fat tire flyers.

8.2 Lush meadows; watch for deer and other wildlife.

9.0 Fenceline and gate.

9.2 Squaw Creek Road; watch for traffic. Turn left and pedal east.

10.1 Turn right onto Rat Lake Road (FR 3112) and coast down to the bridge over Squaw Creek.

10.2 Lean right (a spur road goes left) and uphill. Begin a moderate but well-shaded climb.

10.8 Spur goes right; stay left (signed for Rat Lake, 1 mile).

11.2 FR 3112 makes a big hairpin left. At the apex of the turn take the signed trail on the right over the kelly hump. This wide, rocky route is heavily used by ATVers.

11.5 Old slide area. Ride the narrow singletrack on the uphill side through the slide.

11.6 Turn left on old (closed) logging road. Right goes 0.1 mile to Rat Lake, a pleasant spot for a rest. Continue by returning to the old logging road, which winds through forest east of the lake.

13.3 A wooden post on the right marks an ATV detour. Please stay on the road to prevent erosion.

14.0 Follow the ATV track as it veers right, off the old roadbed, and scampers up a strenuous, loose rocky climb on a finger ridge.

14.2 Grade eases; brief downhill to clearing.

14.3 Resume moderately strenuous climb; some rutted sections.

14.6 Near the top of the ridge, turn left at the sign for Pioneer Lakes Trail 79. (Or detour right and uphill (!) to the summit of Garnet Mountain—see Ride 32.) Going left, the ATV doubletrack drops through a patch of perennial downfall and then beelines southeast through a dense stand of lodgepole pine.

14.7 Boggy spot.

15.3 Climbing slightly, the trail breaks out of the trees and onto an open ridge above Pioneer Lakes to the west. CAUTION: Steep dropoffs to the right of trail; dismount and walk to overlooks. Views extend west into the Spanish Peaks unit of the Lee Metcalf Wilderness. The trail stays just left of the cliff here, rolling over small knobs and winding around clumps of fir.

15.5 Prominent point overlooking Pioneer Lakes.

15.6 Short, steep climb into trees.

15.8 Short drop. Trail then swings east and climbs into an old clearcut.

16.3 As views open up to the north and east, the track widens into an old, overgrown logging road. A wooden post marks the route. From here the road makes a quick descent through young stands of pine.

17.0 The road cuts through a nondescript saddle between two low knobs. Continue the downhill run.

17.7 Another old logging road joins in from the left; lean right (check your speed before hitting this turn: it's slightly off-camber and tends to be loose and sandy). The road drops through more clearcuts, then levels off. Watch for boggy sections on the flats.

18.3 Gate and junction with Line Creek Road (FR 3108). Turn right and push up the steep climb to the top of the Squaw-Swan Divide.

18.7 A sign marks the top of the divide, oddly labeled as the Greek Creek Divide. From here the road narrows to one lane and drops south, with plenty of time to glance up at the ridges and peaks parading south above the Gallatin's deep cut.

20.6 Hairpin turn right.

21.3 Spur goes straight; follow the main road around a hairpin turn left.

21.6 Roadbed of logs for 50 yards. Some boggy spots likely. The grade is nearly level here, through meadows and open stands of Doug fir.

23.0 The road bends left at a rocky outcrop. Expect mudholes spanning the road at regular intervals.

23.3 Grab your brakes for a long downhill run twisting through a series of switchbacks. The tread worsens toward the bottom, with loose gravel and sand sprinkled over the bedrock and ruts.

25.0 Junction with Swan Creek Road (FR 481) and that ice chest full of cold, liquid electrolytes you left in the back seat of the shuttle car.

Flattop Mountain
(Buck Creek Ridge Trail)

Location: 35 miles southwest of Bozeman, about 7 miles south of Big Sky in the Madison Range. ***See map on page 144.***

Distance: 5 to 15 miles up and back.

Time: 1 to 3 hours (depending on total distance); plan at least half a day just to soak up the scenery.

Tread: All ATV-width doubletrack.

Aerobic level: Strenuous; moderate on top.

Technical difficulty: 3 with some sections of 4 and 4+.

Hazards: Yield to other trail users (especially four-wheelers and motorbikes). Keep an eye on the weather—do not attempt

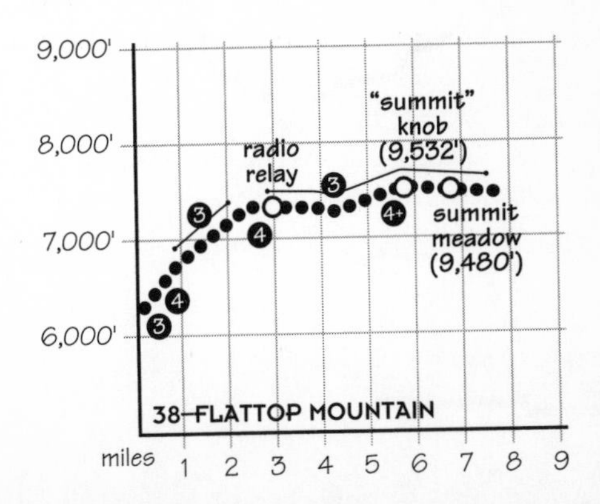

FLATTOP MOUNTAIN
Ride 38

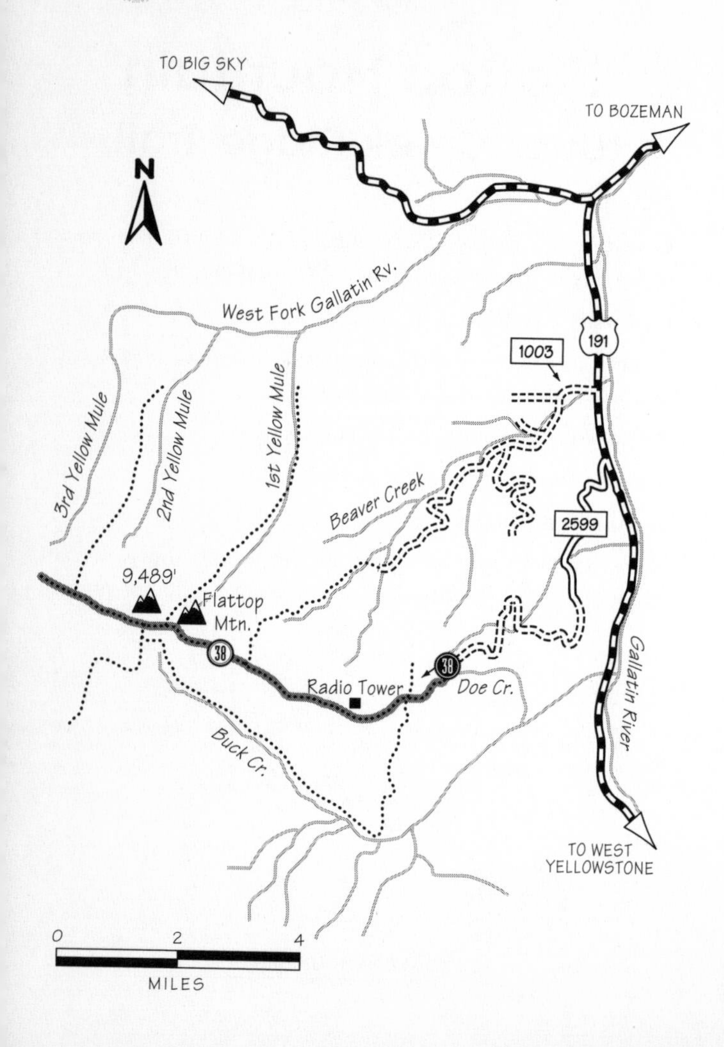

this route if storms are likely. Carry sunscreen and a windbreaker.

Highlights: Mama-where's-my-Kodachrome vistas in all directions; spectacular views from alpine meadows of the Spanish Peaks, Lone Mountain, Cedar Mountain, the Sphinx, the Taylor-Hilgards, the Gallatins, and east to the Absarokas. All this and the trail is a tire-tickler too.

Land status: Gallatin National Forest; Big Sky Lumber.

Maps: Gallatin National Forest; USGS Ousel Falls, Sphinx Mountain.

Access: From Bozeman drive 9 miles west on MT 84 to Four Corners. Turn left onto US 191 and drive 35 miles south to Big Sky. From the Big Sky junction continue 3.8 miles south on US 191 and turn right onto gravel Doe Creek Road (FR 2599). Follow FR 2599 west and south up the flank of the ridge that becomes Flattop Mountain. About 1.7 miles from US 191 a spur road goes right; stay left. Bear right in another mile at the sign for the "parking lot" and Buck Creek. From here, stay on the main road as it winds ever upward through brushy clearcuts and stands of young trees. At 4.7 miles from US 191 the road crosses a well-marked cattleguard and fenceline. Watch for deep ruts at 6.4 miles as the road enters a meadow. The track narrows as it climbs through a few more switchbacks, finally ending atop a scraggly old clearcut, 7.7 miles from US 191. Parking here is limited and there are no trailhead facilities.

The ride:

0.0 Parking area and trailhead. The well-used ATV-width trail climbs west from the parking area into an old clearcut. The grade is moderate but it feels strenuous to most folks. At this elevation (6,300 to 9,500 feet), all of us are flatlanders, gasping for oxygen.

0.3 Cross an old logging track; stay straight on doubletrack.

0.8 Grade eases; rejoin old logging track, which soon goes left and downhill. Bank uphill and right here, resuming moderately strenuous climb on doubletrack.

1.4 Trail skirts the lip of a ridge overlooking the meadows along upper Buck Creek. Great views of the Taylor-Hilgard peaks to the southwest. As the trail swings northwest, the Spanish Peaks and Lone Mountain come into view. Gear down for a few short but steep climbs.

2.3 Grade eases onto the summit ridge. This is the top of the initial climb.

2.7 Solar-powered radio relay and shed on right.

3.0 Trail rolls along open, grassy summit ridge—surprising amounts of gradual downhill—with dramatic views west to the 10,876-foot Sphinx and north to 11,166-foot Lone Mountain.

4.3 Begin moderate climb toward forested knob.

5.0 Grade becomes strenuous, with loose, rocky tread as it enters stand of whitebark pine.

5.3 Grade eases.

5.7 This 9,532-foot knob probably best qualifies as the top of Flattop Mountain, but the views here are blocked by gnarled old pines. Keep pedaling west, through several 4 and 4+ rocky stretches.

6.3 1st Yellowmule trail sign and cairns on right (north). Stay on the main doubletrack bearing west.

6.6 Sign for Slat's Hill leading left (south). Stay right and pedal into...

6.7 Vast grassy meadow on summit of Flattop ridge (9,480 feet). Few other vantage points in the Madisons afford such panoramic views of the entire range, and none but Flattop are accessible by bicycle. To the west and south stretch the southern units of the Lee Metcalf Wilderness, including Cedar Mountain, the Sphinx, Shedhorn and No Man ridges, and Echo Peak and the Taylor-Hilgards. Look north to scan the slopes of Lone Mountain and the Spanish Peaks. And don't neglect the eastern skyline—the Gallatin crest and, in the distance, the spires of Mount Cowen and the Absarokas, nearly 40 miles away as the raven flies. The tread here becomes hummocky with bunchgrass, making for slow going.

7.5 A blazed post marks a good turn-around point. Count on 1 to 1.5 hours to this point and about 45 minutes for the return trip. Watch for sudden rocky drops on the descent (it's tempting to carry too much speed on the smooth sections).

Missouri Headwaters Loop

Location: 29 miles west of Bozeman (3 miles northeast of Three Forks) along the Missouri and Gallatin rivers. ***See map on page 148.***

Distance: 15.3-mile loop.

Time: 1.5 to 2.5 hours.

Tread: 9.4 miles on pavement; 5.9 miles on good gravel road.

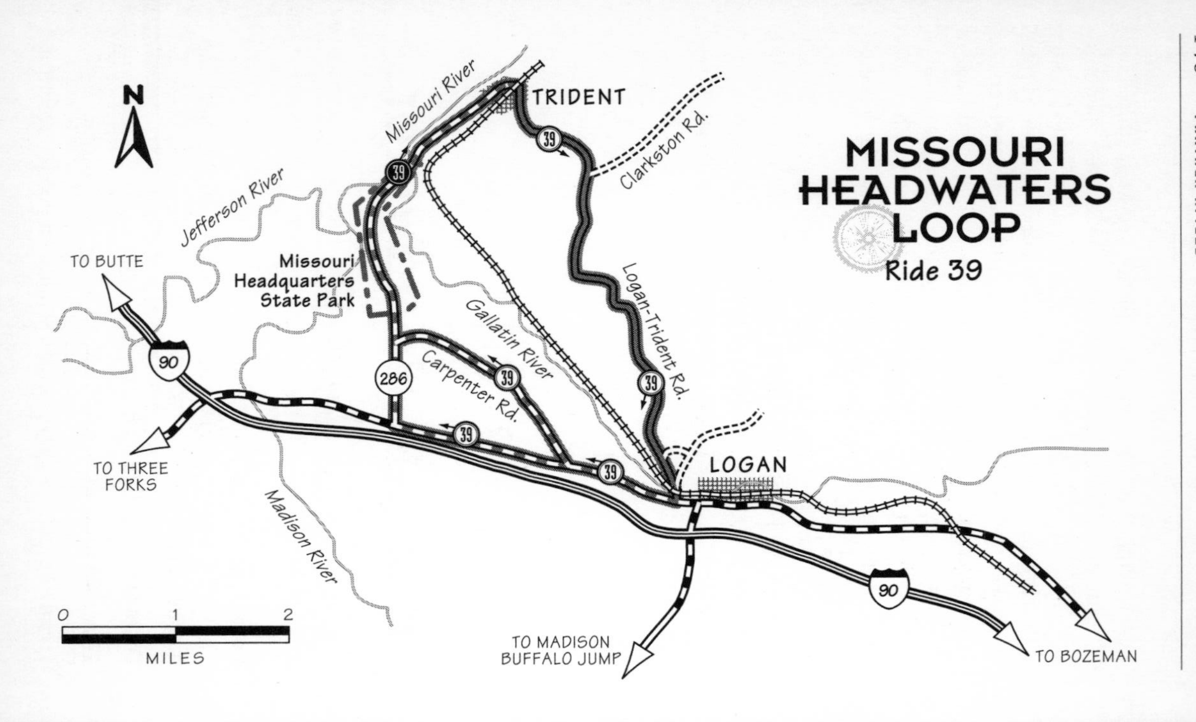
MISSOURI HEADWATERS LOOP
Ride 39
N
TRIDENT
Missouri River
Clarkston Rd.
Jefferson River
TO BUTTE
Missouri Headquarters State Park
Gallatin River
Logan-Trident Rd.
Carpenter Rd.
286
39
90
LOGAN
TO THREE FORKS
Madison River
TO MADISON BUFFALO JUMP
TO BOZEMAN
0
1
2
MILES

Aerobic level: Easy, with one moderate hillclimb.

Technical difficulty: 1.

Hazards: Traffic can be heavy on MT 2 and County Road 286; three railroad crossings.

Highlights: Missouri Headwaters State Park (fishing, hiking, picnicking, interpretive exhibits; river access; expansive views from the Logan-Trident Road; a good year-round ride.

Land status: Private (Holnam, Inc., Cress Springs Ranch); State.

Maps: Montana State Highway Map; USGS Logan.

Access: From Bozeman drive 29 miles west on I-90 to Exit 278 at Three Forks. Turn right and drive 2 miles east on MT 2, then turn left onto County Road 286 at the sign for Missouri Headwaters State Park. Drive 2.9 miles north on CR 286 and park at the Fort Rock interpretive site (0.7 mile past the first Fort Rock sign and access).

The ride:

0.0 Fort Rock. Pedal north on paved CR 286.
0.2 Bridge over Gallatin River.

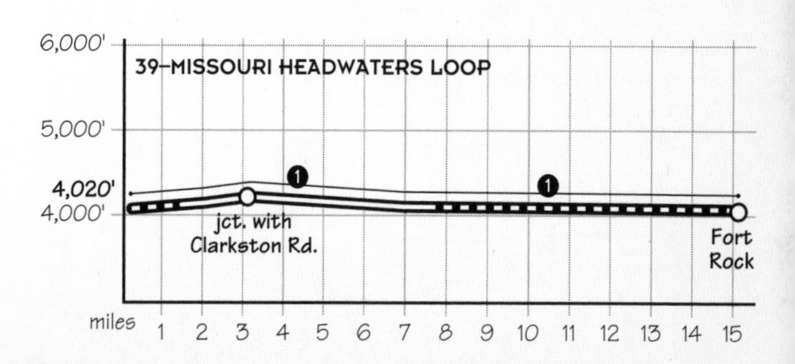

1.2 Enter the "town" of Trident, home of the Holnam talc plant. Watch for free-ranging guard dogs. In Trident the road doglegs right, crosses a set of railroad tracks, and immediately doglegs left (straight ahead dead ends in a parking lot). Follow the road north around the west side of the huge concrete silos.

1.5 Pavement ends, second railroad crossing. Begin 0.6-mile climb through Holnam excavations. CAUTION: Stay on main road; watch for traffic, including large ore trucks. The road—the Logan-Trident Road—eventually tops out on an open bench with views southwest above fertile bottomlands and off to the Tobacco Root Mountains. From here (about 4,229 feet) the road begins a rolling descent to Logan.

3.1 Clarkston Road forks off to left; bear right to stay on the Logan-Trident Road. This stretch of gravel road is usually well-graded and free of washboards. Although wet weather may turn it to gumbo, the road's southwest exposure tends to help it dry out quickly, making this a good early and late-season ride.

6.9 Logan shooting range on the left.

7.2 Railroad crossing.

7.4 Bridge over Gallatin River; turn right onto paved MT 2. CAUTION: watch for high-speed traffic; narrow shoulders. (If traffic is bothersome, turn right in 0.8 mile onto paved Carpenter Road to CR 286.)

12.4 Turn right onto CR 286.

15.3 Fort Rock site.

Appendix A:

Other Bozeman-area Routes

Here's a Pandora's box of "other" roads and trails. The first group offers passable but less than tantalizing rides—they make good alternatives when your favorite trails are full of hikers, downfall, or snow.

The second group of trails is mentioned solely to warn mountain bikers to stay away from them. These routes may be too rocky, steep, erosion-prone, or chronically muddy. If you want to travel these trails, go on foot (call it cross-training) and walk softly.

Alternate routes

Trail Creek Road - 7 miles east of Bozeman, at Exit 316 on I-90. Trail Creek Road (FR 6917) is heavily traveled at times and often full of washboards. But side roads, especially Goose Creek and FR 245 to the Trail Creek cabin, are worth exploring. Some of these roads become impassable when wet.

South Bangtails - About 10 miles east of Bozeman, take the Jackson Creek exit on I-90. Drive about 1.5 miles north and take the right-hand fork to FR 977. This was a popular biking area in the old days, but heavy logging has ruined many routes. Expect unmaintained trails and confusing junctions.

Mount Blackmore - About 16 miles south of Bozeman, park at the trailhead lot on the northwest corner of Hyalite Reservoir. A few hammerhead riders actually enjoy crunching their quads against the climb on Trail 423 to 10,154-foot Mount Blackmore. The early going—about 2.5 miles up to Blackmore Lake—alternates between singletrack and old jeep track. It's often muddy and, on weekends, busy with foot traffic. About 1.3 miles beyond the lake the trail runs into the open flank of Mount Blackmore and becomes increasingly rocky. A challenge even for advanced knobby noggins. Try it, if you are so compelled, but do it on a dry, sunny, mid-week day.

Moose and Portal creeks - About 35 miles south of Bozeman on the east side of US 191 in Gallatin Canyon. Both drainages are pierced by logging roads and some trails. The roads are great for beginning riders who want to get away from town.

Porcupine Creek - About 43 miles south of Bozeman on the east side of US 191, 2.5 miles south of Big Sky. Trails 34 and 160 lead about 11 miles in and up to Ramshorn Lake at the foot of Fortress Mountain. This steady, strenuous climb features plenty of challenges for fit, skilled riders. ATVers—mostly motorbikers—have gouged deep ruts into the trail in places; mud and large, loose rocks are also common. Come out Buffalo Horn Creek if you can arrange a shuttle on US 191. These trails are impassable for bikes after wet weather.

Nixon Gulch - About 23 miles northwest of Bozeman, 5 miles north of Manhattan on Nixon Gulch Road. This moderate track wanders into the sere Horseshoe Hills. Stay on designated routes and obey all private property postings. Roads may be impassable when wet. Watch for rattlesnakes.

Madison River - 37 miles west of Bozeman on MT 84 (Norris Road). Park at the Bear Trap Canyon BLM recreation Area on the south side of MT 84 just before the bridge over the Madison River. From here it's 3 miles south on a rocky but beautiful one-lane road along the Madison to the trailhead for the Bear Trap Wilderness (no bikes allowed beyond this point). Or pedal across the Madison Bridge on MT 84 and north on the west side road. Here you can bump along on a rutted jeep track for about 5 miles (one way) across BLM and state land. The west side road also allows vehicle access for popular fishing and rock climbing spots. Watch for rattlesnakes.

Finally, hundreds of miles of trails and rough roads are waiting to be explored within an hour's drive of Bozeman. Many of these routes see comparatively little traffic, and some have notably longer riding seasons than trails closer to home.

On the east flank of the **Tobacco Root Mountains** Trail 301 climbs west from Pony to Hollowtop Lake at the foot of a 10,604-foot peak of the same name; Willow Creek Road (FR 160) scrambles to the crest of the range.

North on US 89 from Livingston, trails and old roads in the north end of the **Crazy Mountains** and throughout the **Castle Mountains** offer many loop-ride opportunities.

Down the **Paradise Valley of the Yellowstone** try Eightmile Creek and Big Creek for loop or out-and-back rides; Tom Miner Basin allows access to Buffalo Horn Pass and the possibility of dropping out Buffalo Horn Creek to US 191 on the Gallatin.

Also on the **Gallatin,** test your legs against the climb on Trail 6 to Cinnamon Mountain. Or turn west up Taylor Creek Road (FR 134) and venture onto Trail 33 to Albino Lake or the logging roads at the head of the drainage.

Trails NOT Recommended for Mountain Bike Use

Bear Canyon - southeast of Bozeman. Clay soils here and heavy ATV use have combined to leave a highly eroded, ugly track. Bike it only after a long dry spell. Then it makes for a decent loop into Mystic Lake and out Sourdough Creek.

New World Gulch - southeast of Bozeman. This trail is rocky and almost always wet. It's miserable on a bike. Again, it may be more passable after a long dry spell, and then would make a tough but alluring loop ride into Mystic Lake.

Cottonwood Canyon - South of Bozeman. Cottonwood is perhaps the most scenic canyon in the area. And it remains that way in part because the trail is so rocky (bouldery) and rugged. No kidding—it is not bikeable, and the upper section is only worse. Enjoy its beauty in a pair of hiking boots.

Hyalite Lake - South of Bozeman. We're talking about the upper lake here, the one at the base of Hyalite Peak. The trail takes off from Grotto Falls and every year some cyclist is suckered into trying it. But there are numerous steep (!) and technical sections, and the upper basin needs a rest from overuse, especially from hooves and wheels.

Bridger Mountains Trail - North of Bozeman. This trail runs along the crest of the Bridger Range from the M to Hardscrabble Peak. But it's not built for bikes. A few short sections are passable, but most of the trail is incredibly rugged, with long steep (!) grades and extremely rocky tread. Hike or run it as cross-training.

Rat Lake ATV Trail - Above Squaw Creek, down Gallatin Canyon. Please stay off this unofficial trail. It short cuts the switchbacks on the closed logging road, which is the designated route to Garnet Mountain (see rides 32, 33, 37). The Forest Service intends to close the ATV trail to prevent erosion.

Appendix B:

Information Sources

Gallatin National Forest
10 E. Babcock Avenue
P.O. Box 130, Federal Building
Bozeman, MT 59771
(406) 587-6747

Bozeman Ranger District
3710 Fallon Street, Box C
Bozeman, MT 59715
(406) 587-6920

Livingston Ranger District
H.C. 62, Box 3197
Livingston, MT 59047
(406) 222-1892

Montana Department of Fish, Wildlife and Parks
Region 3
1400 South 19th
Bozeman, MT 59715
(406) 994-4042

Outdoor Recreation Program Montana State University
S.O.B. Barn
Bozeman, MT 59717
(406) 994-3621

Bozeman Chamber of Commerce
P.O. Box B
1205 East Main
Bozeman, MT 59715
(406) 586-5421
1-800-228-4224

Bozeman Deaconess Hospital
915 Highland Blvd.
Bozeman, MT 59715
(406) 585-5000
Emergency: 585-1000

Bike Shops

Bangtail Bikes
508 West Main
Bozeman, MT 59715
(406) 587-4905

The Bike Shop (Owenhouse Ace Hardware)
25 South Black Ave.
Bozeman, MT 59715
(406) 587-5404

The Roundhouse
1422 West Main
Bozeman, MT 59715
(406) 587-1258

Chalet Sports
108 West Main
Bozeman, MT 59715
(406) 587-4595

Summit Bike and Ski
26 South Grand
Bozeman, MT 59715
(406) 587-1064

Glossary

ATB: All-terrain bicycle; a.k.a. mountain bike, sprocket rocket, fat tire flyer.

ATV: All-terrain vehicle; in this book ATV refers to motorbikes and three- and four-wheelers designed for off-road use.

Bail: Getting off the bike, usually in a hurry, and whether or not you meant to. Often a last resort.

Bunny hop: Leaping up, while riding, and lifting both wheels off the ground to jump over an obstacle (or for sheer joy).

Clean: To ride without touching a foot (or other body part) to the ground; to ride a tough section successfully.

Contour: A line on a topographic map showing a continuous elevation level over uneven ground. Also a verb indicating a fairly easy or moderate grade: "The trail contours around the west flank of the mountain before the final grunt to the top."

Dab: To put a foot or hand down (or hold onto or lean on a tree or other support) while riding. If you have to dab, then you haven't ridden that piece of trail **clean.**

Downfall: Trees that have fallen across the trail.

Doubletrack: A trail, jeep road, ATV route, or other track with two distinct ribbons of **tread,** typically with grass growing in between. No matter which side you choose, the other rut always looks smoother.

Endo: Lifting the rear wheel off the ground and riding (or abruptly not riding) on the front wheel only. Also known, at various degrees of control and finality, as a nose wheelie, "going over the handlebars," and a face plant.

Fall line: The angle and direction of a slope; the **line** you follow when gravity is in control and you aren't.

Graded: When a gravel road is scraped level to smooth out the washboards and potholes, it has been *graded.* In this book, a road is listed as graded only if it is regularly maintained. Even these roads are not always graded every year.

Granny gear: The innermost and smallest of the chainrings on the bottom bracket spindle (where the pedals and crank arms attach to the bike's frame). Shift down to your granny gear (and up to the biggest cog on the rear hub) to find your lowest ratio for easiest climbing.

Hammer: To ride hard; derived from how it feels afterward: "I'm hammered."

Hammerhead: Someone who actually enjoys feeling **hammered.** A Type A rider who goes hard and fast all the time.

Kelly hump: An abrupt mound of dirt across the road or trail. These are common on old logging roads and skidder tracks, placed there to block vehicle access. At high speeds, they become launching pads that transform bikes into satelites and riders into astronauts.

Line: The route (or trajectory) between or over obstacles or through turns. **Tread** or trail refers to the ground you're riding on; the line is the path you choose within the tread (and exists mostly in the eye of the beholder).

Off-the-seat: Moving your butt behind the bike seat and over the rear tire; used for control on extremely steep descents. This position increases braking power, helps prevent **endos,** and reduces skidding.

Portage: To carry the bike, usually up a steep hill, across unrideable obstacles, or through a stream.

Quads: Thigh muscles (short for quadraceps); or maps in the USGS topographic series (short for quadrangles). The right quads (of either kind) can prevent or get you out of trouble in the backcountry.

Ratcheting: Also known as backpedaling; pedaling backwards to avoid bashing feet or pedals on rocks or other obstacles.

Sidehill: Where the trail crosses a slope's **fall line**. If the **tread** is narrow, keep your uphill pedal up to avoid hitting the ground. If the tread has a sideways slant, you may have to use body english to keep the bike vertical and avoid side-slipping.

Singletrack: A trail, game run, or other track with only one ribbon of **tread.** But this is like defining an orgasm as a muscle cramp. Good singletrack is pure fun.

SPD: A type of pedal with a binding that accepts a matching cleat on the sole of a bike shoe. The cleat locks to the pedal for more control and efficient pedaling, and is easily unlatched safe landings (in theory).

Spur: A side road or trail that splits off from the main route.

Surf: Riding through loose gravel or sand, when the wheels slalom from side to side. Also *heavy surf:* frequent and difficult obstacles.

Suspension: A bike with front suspension has a shock-absorbing fork or stem. Rear suspension absorbs shock between the rear wheel and frame. A bike with both is said to be fully suspended.

Switchbacks: When a trail goes up a steep slope, it zig zags or *switchbacks* across the **fall line** to ease the gradient of the climb. Well-designed switchbacks make a turn with at least an 8-foot radius and remain fairly level within the turn itself. These are rare, however, and cyclists often struggle to ride through sharply angled, sloping switchbacks.

Track stand: Balancing on a bike in one place, without rolling forward appreciably. Cock the front wheel to one side and bring that pedal up to the 1 or 2 o'clock position. Now control your side-to-side balance by applying pressure on the pedals and brakes and changing the angle of the front wheel, as needed. It takes practice but really comes in handy at stoplights, on **switchbacks,** and when trying to free a foot before falling. (See **SPD.**)

Tread: The riding surface, particularly regarding **singletrack.**

Water bar: A log, rock, conveyor belting, ditch or other barrier placed in the **tread** to divert water off the trail and prevent erosion. Peeled logs can be slippery and cause bad falls, especially when they angle sharply across the trail.